ABU TELFAN,

OR,

THE RETURN FROM THE MOUNTAINS OF THE MOON.

BY

WILHELM RAABE.

TRANSLATED FROM THE GERMAN BY

SOFIE DELFFS.

"If you knew what I know," said Mahomet, "you would weep much and laugh little."

IN THREE VOLUMES.
VOL. III.

LONDON:
CHAPMAN AND HALL, LIMITED,
HENRIETTA STREET, COVENT GARDEN.

1882.

ABU TELFAN.

CHAPTER I.

In his study sat Professor Christian George Reihenschlager, occupied with the study of comparative philology, and in her room sat Miss Serena Reihenschlager, likewise occupied with a kind of comparative science. It was a bright afternoon in January, the sun looked gaily if not warmly in through the windows, but neither the professor's nor his daughter's soul were as bright as the day. Over both souls there lay a delicate veil; not the grey veil of ill-humour, or the yellow veil of annoyance, but rather the blue-tinted one of a vague, not unpleasant longing after a merry and entertaining companion, who was

B

absent on a journey, and whose empty place
at the afternoon coffee - table had already
given rise to various allusions and observations.

"Quite apart from the Coptic grammar, it
is really a very good sign, with regard to the
young man's character, that we miss him so
much, even after so short an acquaintance,"
the professor had said ; and Serena, playing
with the sugar-tongs, had replied—

"Well, I don't know about his being so
very young, but I too like him very well.
He is extremely entertaining, and has soon
found out that I am not averse to laughter,
and know how to appreciate a jest at the
right time. What would otherwise become
of such a dry and learned existence ? Yes,
hitherto we have got on very well together,
and, considering that the great washing-day
is happily once more a thing of the past, I
thought I might indulge in the luxury of a
comfortable chat, for which purpose I have

sent for the pasha to come here and replace
his master. Oh, dear, dear! I really should·
like to know what heaven intended with me,
when it placed me in the midst of this
African, Coptic, and Indian menagerie, for I
confess that I am utterly in the dark about
it."

" *Om!* " said the professor, fixing both his
eyes intently on the tip of his nose, and then
he once more climbed up, in dressing-gown
and slippers, to his own dominions. He but
rarely attended the audiences which his
daughter gave; and with regard to the pasha,
it is true that he esteemed him as a human
being, but otherwise he felt himself too much
above him in clearness of perception of the
world in general, to bestow even a fragment
of his precious time on him.

Om! With blinking eyes Täubrich sat
on the utmost edge of a chair, and in a
rocking-chair opposite, also with blinking
eyes, sat the little inquisitor, playing a tune

with her finger - tips on the table beside
her.

"So, Täubrich, you are likewise convinced
that your master has a good heart?"

"Oh, Fräulein!" sighed the tailor, "what
regards his intellect, I can only guess at it,
for a man like myself could never fathom it;
but his heart I know from both sides, as well
as any coat that I ever had to turn. His
heart is true and genuine on both sides, for
how could he else condescend to befriend me,
me, who was brought home by the police, and
who does not even know at the present moment
how it all came about. I well know what I
am and what he is. Many a one has told
me that my head is not quite right, but he
never did. Am I a toy? Am I a poor
crazy fool that is good for nothing except to
be the butt of everybody? The whole world
says so, but he does not. I believe that he
feels sorry for me, which, though it is not
at all necessary, yet pleases me very much.

Still, at other times, I again think that this is
not all, and I say to myself, 'It is not from
mere pity, Täubrich, that he befriends you;
but he does it for companionship, when he
sits down beside you of an evening, or in the
middle of the night, and talks to you, as he
would to any other reasonable being, and
unburdens all his good and wise heart to
you.'"

"Indeed? Does he do that, Täubrich?"
asked the young lady. "That is most
curious and very good of him. If your coffee
is not sweet enough the sugar-bowl stands
beside you to the left, near your elbow. So
he unburdens all his good and wise heart to
you, and you understand what he says?"

"By no means!" said the pasha, with
great emphasis. "To be sure, sometimes it is
as if I were looking through a chink in the
blue mist that surrounds me, but this does
not last. You see, I cannot get rid of Damascus and Jerusalem, that is the mischief;

but after all it does not matter much, for if one of two persons only knows what he wants, it is enough for both."

"Oh, Täubrich!" sighed Fräulein, meditatively, but she might just as well have sighed, "Oh, Ferdinand!" or something similar.

"Well, you see, Miss, I have been a poor orphan all the days of my life, so to say, and a tailor is altogether no man who inspires mankind with any respect, if he does not come with a long bill. And I have never been more than a tailor's workman, for I had a certain striving after something higher, and so I came to the heavenly Orient, to Jerusalem and far into the desert and the land of palms, just as my patron, Mr. Hagebucher, got to the remotest part of Africa. And then I found myself suddenly once more in my native country, before my mother's door—people say, transported there by the police, but to me it all seems like magic, and from this I have never been able quite to recover; but I have remained as in a dream, and I suppose I shall ever remain in it. People say that I had better have been deposited at the door of a madhouse, and most of them may have the right to say so, but not all; and what regards myself, I sometimes think that a griffin must have put me on some high mountain, or how could Mr. Hagebucher else have found me and become my friend? Lieutenant Kind does not seem to be at all surprised at this, and that is a comfort to me."

"Kind? Kind? Who is this Lieutenant Kind?" asked Serena.

"He is, as I said before, also an acquaintance of mine, but not one made in the land of palms or on a mountain top, but a brannew acquaintance, not at all pleasant to me."

"You seem to have a great many acquaintances, Täubrich."

"So I have. On this and that side of the

Mediterranean; on this and that side of the
clouds. Ah, Fräulein, you sit here in your
pretty room, and for an inhabitant of the
Kesselstrasse it seems like a fairy-tale that
the sun coming in through the windows can
shine, even in winter, on such green bushes
and flowers. It is very pretty, and I hope
will remain so; and it would be very ill if
you were to know more about the world, and
the evil acquaintances that one can make
there, than your linnet over there in its cage.
Here I also feel at ease, and my eyes to-day
are clear enough, but in a few minutes, or in
an hour after I have shut this door behind
me, all is changed again. May God protect
your bright eyes, Fräulein, for—for every
one thing that we know since we have begun
to exist, there are twenty things around us
that are a greater mystery than the creation
of the universe, and there is no trust to be
placed in smiles or tears, in an open, or a
clenched hand. When you walk along the

houses you do not know what is going on inside; and if you should happen to cast a look through the windows, there are back rooms and dark closets into which you are certainly not permitted to gaze, and it is well that it is so. You sit safe and snug in your bright little room, and should remain in it as long as possible. When you are once outside you have no other choice than my palms or those of Mr. Leonhard, or a madhouse. So it is, and the proof is that the professor, my kind master upstairs, in his study between his hieroglyphics and pyramids and obelisks, knows this quite well; but you must not tell him that I said so, for he thinks but little of my intellect."

"But Lieutenant Kind thinks more of it, doesn't he? About as much as Mr. Hagebucher?"

"No, no, miss! You see, the lieutenant comes from a very different country than my patron. He has nothing whatever to do with

palm-trees and mountain-heights. Lieutenant
Kind is an acquaintance such as one makes
at night in some evil dream; and if such
acquaintances are able to produce a great
fear, a shivering and trembling then, this is
nothing compared to the surprise when they
step into one's room in the morning, in the
flesh, and bid you a good-day like any other
ordinary mortal, though in a manner of their
own. We take an interest in each other,
the lieutenant and I, that is, he does so more
in me, ever since the day after the lecture;
that is, when he came in the dark night,
asking for Mr. Hagebucher, and waited for
him in my room."

"I suppose that he brought Mr. Leonhard the news of his father's death?" said
Serena.

"I do not think so. Mr. Leonhard, may
be intentionally, left the matter in darkness,
in the letter which he wrote to me, as well
as in that to your father, Fräulein."

"This I would consider very unkind in him, for I really think that we always showed perfect confidence in the gentleman," cried Serena, with a shrug of her shoulders; but Täubrich Pasha only shook his head meditatively and said—

"Do not excite yourself, Fräulein. As I said before, you sit warm and snug here. If I were you I would not stir, but remain in my hiding-place as quiet as a little mouse."

"And come out at night when everybody is abed, to visit the pantry and steal sugar! No, thanks, Master Täubrich Pasha, I really feel no inclination to become a linnet, a bullfinch, or a canary bird. And now tell me something more of Lieutenant Kind."

"He has often come to the Kesselstrasse, after having once found his way thither," said Täubrich; "and he has also invited me to come and see him, and I went, but it is not at all pleasant there, as it makes me shiver all over, ever so long afterwards."

"But you converse together, and speak of this and that?"

"To be sure, and if I may mention it, we each smoke a pipe and sit opposite each other, neither speaking a word; I, because I have nothing to say, and the lieutenant probably because he does not want to speak."

"That must be most interesting!" Serena cried, laughingly.

"Oh, no, it is not interesting," said the pasha; "but at all events it is far pleasanter than when the lieutenant is in his talkative mood, and takes a pleasure in making my flesh creep all over. Pleasure did I say? Well, to be sure, he does not look as if he were enjoying himself particularly, but still he does it with a sort of relish."

"And of what does he speak, Täubrich?"

"He talks to me of his late wife and his late daughter, and of a lot of people, both dead and living, and in a way which can

never agree with a poor tailor, though he
has been in Jerusalem and Damascus, and
has been fighting all his life with Turks,
Bedouins, Jews, and Christians of all descrip-
tions. Also I am firmly persuaded that when
he is in this mood he does not think of my
presence, but believes that he is talking to
the walls. Ah, Fräulein, for a man who fell
asleep at Mar Saba in the valley of Kidron,
and awoke again in the Kesselstrasse, he
has a way about him, which might easily
compromit that man with a high-born aris-
tocracy and a worshipful public, for one would
like to cry out aloud like some frightened
child, and ask to be taken home, away from
this bad, dirty, bloody shame and misery.
Then it is as if sun, moon, and stars were
made up of mud and blood, and then pitched
into endless space, and as if from the lowest
depth to the greatest height there was
nothing but sin and death. Ah, my dear
lady, do not you mind Lieutenant Kind and

his stories, but let us rather speak of Mr.
Hagebucher, or send me home."

Serena Reihenschlager had long abandoned
her negligent, lounging position on the rocking-chair. Bounding forward, and resting
both her arms on the table, she gazed at the
tailor, full of surprise, and then said—

"Täubrich, if I did not consider you a
very harmless man, I would indeed wish you
a good evening, and, after I had locked my
door, think all sort of queer things about
you. But let it be, for I have no wish to
meddle with the murderous tales of that old
ware-wolf, or your own wild fancies, especially as dusk is already setting in. Let us
speak of your African master, if that suits
you better. He, no doubt, would succeed in
making me laugh even at midnight and in a
churchyard. By the way, Täubrich, how
old do you think that good man to be ? "

"Compared with his fate, he is a mere
youth, but otherwise I believe he must be

about forty," said the pasha; and Serena, drawing herself up yet a little more, began to tap her right little foot on the floor, to count off the ominous number, but soon giving it up, she laughed softly and merrily.

"Forty! Really a very solid and reasonable age! But what on earth do you call his fate, compared to which you consider him a mere youth? Surely not his stay amongst the Moors? Bah! What is that, for instance, compared to *my* fate?"

"Your fate? Oh, Fräulein, do not utter such heedless speeches!"

"Not at all, friend Täubrich Pasha. Have I not fallen amongst heathens and Moors, as no other woman on God's earth ever did before? Has ever any other woman led such a dull and eventless existence as I have hitherto? I really should like to see her! What does the Egyptian dictionary and the Coptic grammar concern me? I ought to have been born in an ant-hill, but not in the

house of my dear papa, who, in the first
instance, is far too learned, and, secondly,
far too good for me. Oh, Heavens! have I
only been placed into this world, first to
bring about order, and then to be disgusted
with my work? Täubrich, you are the right
person for me! With you, one can talk
without fear of making oneself ridiculous and
of being laughed at for one's frankness. You
are a feeling man, with whom one can chat
very pleasantly; and then you have been in
the Orient. You are the only one who
understands me, without afterwards making
impertinent comments behind my back.
Hark! what was that?"

"The whistle of the locomotive at the
station, Fräulein."

"Of course! The whistle of the Francfort
express. Oh, I know my railway itinerary
by heart, and that is my misery. In former
times, romantic times, the ladies stood on
their balconies, and saw the moon rise or set,

and their knight, or somebody else, who arrived or departed, blew his horn in the woods below. Later on, one listened to the post-horn, and had one's thoughts the while, and, to confess the truth, I think there was more sense in this, for I do not believe much in the romantic days of knighthood. At the present times, we have the whistle of the locomotive for our longing, wandering thoughts, and this latter is by far the most exciting for an anxious, longing heart, especially when the station is not too far off. 'Time to get in, ladies and gentlemen!' Oh, Täubrich, there is a train which leaves soon after midnight, which frequently finds me still awake, and which will yet drive me mad, or make me run away. In the silent night one can also hear the porter's bell quite distinctly, and that puts an end to all romance, and I humbly beg not to be bothered with, 'Hurrying clouds, sailing so high;' or, 'If I were a little bird,' or the like sentimentalities, which nobody any longer believes in."

"These are certainly feelings which a susceptible man experiences at certain periods of his life," said the dreamy tailor, with a deep sigh. "I know that well enough; and there is no doubt that if one be not very careful, these things may carry one far beyond the point one contemplated at first. I know full well whither it took me and Mr. Leonhard, but I really cannot imagine where you should have made such experiences."

"If you were to try and find it out, it would really be very kind of you, and I should feel most grateful. I myself have meditated profoundly on the matter, but I suspect that I might have employed my time more profitably."

The pasha at this moment looked exactly as he did when he least troubled himself with the affairs of the old maid *Europa*.

His eyes assumed a fixed, glassy stare, whilst he muttered—

"For instance, there is the beautiful Miss von Einstein, who had to marry the Baron von Glimmern. *She* sailed with the clouds, and people stood in the streets, making wry mouths as they pointed at the pavement; and they knew exactly where the proud forehead of that woman was yet to lie. Ah, Fräulein!"

"Täubrich," whispered Serena Reihenschläger, "now we have come back to the point where we were before. And we are quite alone, so please tell me something of your dreams. I promise not to tell tales out of school, but I should like to know so much what Mr. Leonhard Hagebucher and that strange lady were doing together at Bumsdorf. I know that they gathered violets and lilies of the valley, and led lambs by silken, rose-coloured ribbons through the meadows. The Fräulein rode on a white horse called Prospero, and Mr. Hagebucher

ran breathlessly by her side. Then there is
another mysterious lady, a hermit, living in
a crumbling old mill, and all this is so near
that one might touch it with one's hand, and
yet one knows nothing about it. So please
tell me of it, my kind Täubrich; my sweetest
Täubrich Pasha. What do you know of all
these mysteries which Mr. Hagebucher ought
to have told us about himself?"

"Hush, hush, Fräulein!" whispered the
pasha. "Let alone the lilies and violets, the
lambs and the meadows. I see a house, a
stately mansion, here in this town, and you
also know it, Miss Reihenschlager. A heavy,
merciless fist comes down. I see mirrors
shivered in their golden frames, and chande-
liers are extinguished. I hear voices, and a
mocking laughter behind me—one voice is
like a wail of despair, and another like a
terrible curse. I fancy that I am on the
fourth gallery in the theatre, during the fifth
act of 'Wallenstein's Death.' Schiller well

knew what he was about when he had that corpse carried across the stage, wrapped up in a carpet; and one need not be a tailor, to feel that scene in every limb. That makes an impression, Fräulein, just as before, when one heard the gate forced open by the conspirators and—— ”

Here Serena uttered a loud cry, and the tailor held fast to his chair with both hands; for in that moment the door, had not been forced open as by Devereux and Macdonald, but somebody had audibly knocked at it, and as neither of the two chatterboxes was able to say, “ Come in,” the knock was repeated still more audibly.

“ Oh, Heavens! Come—in! ” Serena at last managed to say, whilst the pasha stood bolt upright, leaning against the wall; and the door was gently opened, and with a bright smile on his face, Mr. Leonhard Hagebucher looked in, and politely asked—

“ May I enter, Miss Reihenschlager ? ”

"Well, you did startle me! Must you ever come at the wrong moment," cried Serena, with a laugh, but, nevertheless, slightly vexed.

CHAPTER II.

"AND if there isn't my Täubrich! And the professor, no doubt, is upstairs, hard at work; and, in the sweat of his brow, digging for roots. Everything is in its right place; and outside, before the house, I found a wretched black incubus, holding his head with both hands, and sobbing angrily; and on the stair-case I met two little goblins, with turned-up sleeves, who said, 'That blackguard has been well served, and we have turned him out, with all his cobwebs, broken crockery, and other rubbish; but it has cost a deal of trouble.' Well, it is a real pleasure, Miss Serena, to come home on such a cold day, and to be able to warm oneself at such a glowing stove."

"Put some more wood on the fire, Täubrich, and then you can go and tell papa that
Mr. Hagebucher has come back, and that he
is but little changed," laughed Serena; and
Täubrich Pasha, who at that moment might
just as well have been called Gander * Pasha,
for he alternately stood on his right and his
left leg, shot out of the room, and rushed
upstairs. Then a heavy chair was pushed
back upstairs, and there followed a clatter as
if the forty-five folios of the *Thesaurus anti-
quitatum* had fallen from the book-shelves,
followed by the encyclopædia from Master
Peter van der Aa to the learned doctors
Grocoius and Gronovius. Then there was
another rumbling on the staircase; and a
moment later, Professor Reihenschlager rushed
into his daughter's room, seized his African
friend by the neck with both his lean hands,
and cried—

"*Salve! Salve!* All the morning I felt a

* Täubrich in German means a male pigeon.

tickling sensation at my diaphragm; but I
put it on the weather. God be thanked that
you are back, Leonhard! I am stuck fast in
the dialects of Sudan, and I get a very fever
when I only think of the Somali tongue. Of
the girl yonder I will say nothing, as I did
not pay much attention to her, to confess the
truth; but Täubrich has been more dazed
than ever, since you went away. It was
really not nice of you, Hagebucher, to disappear thus, hardly giving us notice, and
forsaking science in such an unwarrantable
fashion. Well, you had better come up at
once to my room, as I have a good many
things to show you, sure to interest you
exceedingly."

"Bravo, papa! That's right; go on!"
cried Serena. "The poor man comes straight
from the railway, as cold as an icicle, and
carries a temperature about him, which he
might show for money under the equator.
Besides, he has buried his poor father at

home, and left his mother and sister behind
in great affliction, and here you receive him
with your grammar and Sudan dialects, as if
in all the world there was nothing more
important for him to do than to hunt up
words for you. Oh, papa, in all my life I
have not met with such selfishness!"

"That is true; I forgot all about it," said
the professor, very crestfallen. "I heartily
beg your pardon, Leonhard. You come back
from your journey half-frozen, and have met
with a very sad loss in your family. Täubrich
can fetch us a bottle of wine out of the cellar;
the child will provide a good supper, and
you, Leonhard, know, without my repeating
it, that we take a very sincere interest in all
that regards you. So I hope you will tell us
all about your journey and your stay at
home; and we will sympathize with you, and
try to comfort you to the best of our ability.
Ay, ay; let us discuss family matters to-day,
and then to-morrow we can start afresh, and
proceed on the path of science."

" You are incorrigible, papa," said Serena ; but Leonhard nevertheless cordially shook hands with the professor, and then with Serena, nor was the pasha forgotten. And the professor's programme for the evening was also carried out, as comfort, as well as sad memories, found their place therein.

Serena let down the window-blinds with her own dainty hands; the bronze Indian girl, who every evening bore the light in a frosted glass globe, was put on the table by Täubrich; the tea-kettle began to sing, the professor to hum, and Leonhard to relate of Nippenburg and Bumsdorf; of his mother and little sister; of his dead father and the living Cousin Wassertreter; but not of the cats'-mill, Mrs. Claudine, or Mr. van der Mook. And Miss Serena Reihenschlager was full of sympathy, and had many a question to ask. The professor, as may be imagined, tried more than once to turn the conversation on the Coptic; but, quickly

becoming aware of the utter uselessness and
inappropriateness of these trials, he asked
pardon, even before a shrug of his daughter's
shoulders reminded him of the mistake he
had made.

There was so much to think and to speak
of, without its being necessary to go back to
comparative philology and the Egyptian
dictionary. Mr. van der Mook was as yet
perfectly superfluous at the Reihenschlager's
tea-table, and that nothing whatever of importance had happened in the Residence
during Leonhard's absence, did not make the
conversation flag. The lecture held in the
halls of the *Harmonie*, which had ended so
unharmoniously, now became an inexhaustible
theme for conversation, which took a different
colouring in everybody's mind, and, with
regard to which, even the professor had something to say which bore no relation to the
subject nearest his heart. In fact, after the
events of these latter days, the lecture was

nothing more than a pleasant theme for a comfortable chat for our African. Even Lieutenant Kind's darkling figure only ventured to step once more into the foreground when it struck eleven, and was time to bid good-bye, after which Leonhard went to the kitchen, there to fetch the pasha.

"He is really a nice—a very agreeable and clever man, and that he seems not to have the slightest idea of his own merits with regard to science, would endear him still more to me, if that were possible. I shall certainly sleep much better now that I know he is back. Good-night, Serena."

"Good-night, papa," said the daughter, but without looking at the old gentleman. When he was gone, she remained sitting for some time before her table, resting her fine forehead on both her hands. An unmistakable resemblance to her father, when he was most absorbed in comparative philology, became visible on her pretty face. Serena was also comparing something, and that most thoroughly; but she, too, stuck fast in her subject, no less than the excellent scholar in his Sudan dialects and Somali language.

"It is really too bad," cried Fräulein, half angrily and half tearfully, but the next moment she raised her head to listen. It struck midnight, and the last stroke of the clock had hardly died out when the train, going off in a south-western direction, sent over its shrill departing whistle. A faint, half-pouting smile passed over Serena's face, and then she said energetically—

- "Now I know what to do. I'll go to bed, and will not trouble my head any longer about it."

This she did, but when she had arranged her pillow to her satisfaction, and pulled the bedclothes over herself, she drowsily muttered between a blush and a yawn—

"For all that, I would like to know what Täubrich Pasha will tell the other fool about

me to-night, and what that other will say
to it."

We, who accompanied the two on their
way to the Kesselstrasse, know this, and are
not justified in withholding this curious conversation from our readers.

"Oh, Sidi, those are a pair of sweet eyes,"
said the tailor, winding up a long inward
soliloquy with these words, addressed to
Hagebucher.

"Yes."

"Like the gleam of a clear brook through
a lovely green wood! And when she opens
her mouth and says, with a dimple in her
right cheek and one in her left, and another
in her chin, 'Mr. Täubrich, I am very glad
to see you so well, this is just as—as if——' "

"Spare yourself the comparison, my friend.
What is the use of bothering over similes?
Let the brook gleam and sparkle, and hold
your tongue."

"Oh, sir, in a caravansary at Jaffa, I once

heard a relater of fairy-tales say, that to
have good music, four instruments were required, a violin, a lute, a cithern, and a harp;
that for a truly pretty nosegay, four kinds of
flowers were needed, roses, myrtles, gilly-
flowers, and lilies; and for a happy life, wine,
money, youth, and love. But *I* think that
with these eyes, a man would have all, music,
flowers, and all that was necessary for a
happy life, and need not mind the rest."

"All that which intoxicates is forbidden,"
sighed Hagebucher.

"That is also my opinion. Meanwhile we
talked a good deal about you, Mr. Leonhard."

"Bismillah! What did she say of me?"
asked Hagebucher, with such vehemence
that the terrified tailor had almost sunk
down on the nearest corner-stone. "You
will have talked a deal of nonsense together,
I warrant! Well, out with it. What does
the dear child think of Africa and the man
from Tumurkieland?"

"Ah, Sidi, we often sat comfortably together in her pretty little room at twilight,
and then—then—well, 'tis strange that I
cannot express it in words, what we said
about you. It is most wonderful! My soul
and my memory are quite filled with it, and
now I know nothing else but that she is
indescribably arch and pretty; but we did
speak of you, Mr. Leonhard, and of the railway, and longings after the distance, and
a hundred other things. But most of all, we
spoke of our dreams and Nippenburg and
Bumsdorf."

The African laughed.

"Don't take any further trouble, Täubrich.
Your account is all that could be desired.
Moreover, we have reached our tent. Blessed
be our entrance, and, let us not become con-
ceited, no matter what ray of light the gods
may cast at our feet. Go to bed, Täubrich
Pasha, and dream, as you live when waking.
I have no better wish for you."

They stood before their house-door ; but, for the present, Leonhard Hagebucher was not allowed to betake himself to his rest.

" I heard of your arrival already at the station," said the ex-Lieutenant Kind, and so I waited for you here. Welcome, Mr. Hage-bucher."

The tailor pressed himself against the wall, and Leonhard said gloomily—

" You are as punctual as the devil when time is up. Well, well. Be welcome too, for I suppose I must say so much for polite-ness' sake! What can I do for you? Is the alarum-bell to sound at the house of Baron von Glimmern even this night? Nobody will prevent you. Forward, forward! Let all your dogs loose, and be you the first on the spot. That, which does not belong to you, you will have to leave for our hands."

" You ought not to speak to me in this way, Mr. Hagebucher," said the lieutenant. " You, least of all, have any cause for this."

"No, no, Kind, you are right. You held your part of the contract, and we will stick to ours. And now tell me what you want with me at this late hour. Won't you come up?"

The old man shook his head.

"It becomes ever more difficult for me to breathe shut up between four walls, and, moreover, I shall not detain you long. Let us remain in the open air."

Leonhard pushed the pasha into the house, and shut the door behind him. Then, putting his arm into that of the old man, he walked with him through the Kesselstrasse, but in less than a quarter of an hour he returned, slowly climbing up to the fourth storey, and, vehemently dashing his hat to the ground, he laughed bitterly and angrily—

"So that's what he wants, is it? He demands to have Mr. van der Mook to bring the tragedy to an end! Like a galley-slave who has lost his comrade to whom he was chained, he asks for his companion. The iron ball proves too heavy for him. By God, he shall make an end as he can, and nobody shall lend him a helping hand! An eye for an eye, a tooth for a tooth! The way is open before him, so why does he stop and look round, instead of making straight for his laudable aim? He has nothing, nothing whatever to do on the path that leads to Mrs. Claudine! What does it regard those who found this path, whether the knife trembles in his hand or not?"

He cast an excited look around the room. The tailor had lighted a fire in the stove, and placed a burning lamp on the table. For the first time since his deliverance from the mud cabins of Abu Telfan, Leonhard Hagebucher took notice of the dirty walls, the low ceiling, of his present abode, and made a wry face at them. He felt old, chilly, in a bad humour, and had a strong craving after light, rest, and cleanliness. It was but yesterday that he had taken leave of Mrs. Claudine, and already to-day he missed her deeply and sadly, and in vain searched all the corners of his philosophical system for some compensation for her calming presence, and her grand, silent wisdom. For a few short moments he had been allowed to forget his own uncomfortable existence in Serena's cosy little room, but, hard and remorseless, Lieutenant Kind destroyed this brief happiness, and instead of taking it with him into his dreams, our African could only sit down on the edge of his bed, and stow away the gains and losses of these last weeks in the different receptacles of his memory.

There was no doubt the old gentleman in Bumsdorf was dead and buried, and the prodigal son now reigned in his stead. Cousin Wassertreter had compared an inventory of all the goods and chattels with the existing reality, and found everything in the most perfect order, without being one bit surprised.

In Nippenburg, people had long known
that Inspector Hagebucher, being well up in
arithmetic and agriculture, had saved a good
lump of money, and merely regretted that the
handsome fortune was to fall into such
unworthy hands.   This last consideration
seemed to be a matter of perfect indifference
to Providence, who had well taken care of the
African adventurer's mother and sister; and
once more it became evident that a man,
belonging to the gentry of Nippenburg,
might leave the stage without putting the
world the least bit out of the old track.
However, it is but fair to mention that since
the death of Hagebucher senior, Hagebucher
junior appeared in a much more favourable
light in the eyes of Nippenburg; and by this
time there were quite a number of people
who began to pardon him all the excitement,
commotion, and disappointments which he had
caused in his native place by his unexpected
reappearance, and who even made some weak

efforts to raise him in public opinion, as a
man who, though rather " odd," was yet on
the whole quite respectable. All this, however, was likewise a matter of perfect indifference to our friend Leonhard, and with
a hasty wave of his hand he dismissed the
inventory, as well as the glossaries made
thereon, from his mind.

The snow-covered mill in the valley!
That, and all the thoughts connected with it,
worried the African far more just at present
than his quiet, though mournful, home. To
be sure, mother and son were quite contented
there for the moment; and if an impenetrable
hedge of thorns and brambles had grown up
around the mill, as around the palace of the
sleeping beauty, none but a very unreasonable
soul would have desired anything better for
its two inhabitants. But how long could the
secret be kept? Cousin Wassertreter knew
of it, and had promised to keep good watch
over it; but, was it possible to exclude

Nippenburg, Bumsdorf, and Fliegenhausen, even till the snow would melt?

And what if the low murmur should swell into a cry? If a voice were suddenly to whisper into Nicola von Glimmern's ear, 'The dead have returned after all'? Her place of refuge was prepared in the cats'-mill for poor Nicola, but could she fly thither with that word in her ear? Would the name of Victor Fehleysen not drive her back into the furthest distance?

Nowhere could he discover a way out of his perplexity. The air seemed to suffocate him. He jumped up, opened the window, and leant out.

"The coward!" he exclaimed, grinding his teeth, and, strange to say, by this he meant Lieutenant Kind.

His thoughts followed the lieutenant's retreating figure through the night. His hands moved convulsively as if he held some invisible threads by which he directed the

old man according to his will. He accompanied
him from street to street; step after step, he
followed close at his heels to the threshold of
that house which had cast its dark shadow
over all his European life.

He saw him—he saw how he stretched out
his hand towards the bell-pull; he would
have recognized the shrill, startling sound of
that bell, if he had been miles away. With
another curse, this time not directed against
Lieutenant Kind, he stretched out his arm
as if he would hold back the hard bony hand
of fate. Ah, let her sleep but one—one night
longer!

Closing the window, he stepped back and
flung himself once more on his bed; but now
there could no longer be any question of
clear thought, of sober, dispassionate reflection
over his gains and losses.

At the edge of the wood sat the fair Nicola
von Einstein, weaving a garland of the
flowers that lay in her lap, and singing—

" *Debout* ye knights and pages,
  'Tis time to throw your gages,
  Now come from far and near;
  And all their hearts they flutter,
  Yet not a word they utter,
  Clymenè has appear'd."

What a vain world! ´No thought, no wish, no intention that can be held fast, beyond the next quarter of an hour. Was the dull brooding in captivity at Abu Telfan, or the wild, senseless rushing out into the world of Mr. van der Mook, not preferable to this vain fretting and tormenting, this feverish search after what was right, Mrs. Claudine? Who gets anything else but his deserts in this world? So let everybody meet his fate. Who is so stupid as to stir, unless the whip is raised over his back? And who is fool enough, after so many thousand years of experience, still to play the knight-errant, and try to set right the heads and hearts of mankind?

The happiest, the least guilty, will ever be he who passes his life in a dream like

Täubrich Pasha; but those who are not so blessed had best retire into that selfishness which leaves its neighbour unmolested, and builds its nest of the feathers, the cotton, and blades of grass which lie about in the world at everybody's disposal. We but lately uttered some fine words in the cats'-mill, Mrs. Claudine Fehleysen, and, in spite of all confusion and evil, the world lay before us in a soft, radiant light. But this was in the cats'-mill, in the middle of the wood, where even the gentle murmuring waters were no longer counting the hours. There you sit also in a dream, Mrs. Claudine; but what shall a man do here in the Grand-ducal Residence, where Lieutenant Kind sits *in natura* on Mrs. Nicola's threshold?

"I sleep with a sword under my pillow!" cried Leonhard, excitedly; but when sleep at last really came to him, he dreamt of a warm dressing-gown, a pair of warm slippers, a long pipe, and a singing tea-kettle.

CHAPTER III.

" COME in."

With a nervous strain, Hagebucher had listened to the hasty footsteps coming up his staircase and stopping before his door, but with all the greater pleasure he then received his early visitor, who turned out to be nobody else than the lieutenant, Mr. Hugo von Bumsdorf, the merry son of a well-providing father.

" I have just heard of your return from our sweet home," said the youthful warrior, " and I thought it my duty to come at once, to assure you of my heartfelt sympathy. You have lost your papa, as mine wrote to me, in a rather melancholy letter; and, as I said before, I heartily condole with you, though I may add that the affection which the old gentleman bore me, was never so deep as that I entertained for him."

"I thank you for your sympathy, Herr von Bumsdorf," replied Leonhard. "Your family are all well, and have charged me with their kindest messages."

"Thanks," said the lieutenant, not the least bit moved. "Has the governor given you nothing else for me?"

"Yes," said Hagebucher, smilingly; "but it is something which—— "

"Which is more in the patriarchal line, such as 'Campe's fatherly advice to his daughter;' something in the ethical and moral style! Oh, don't mention it, my dear fellow! If this my Arcadian begetter only knew how every day, every hour, preaches to me here, he would most certainly keep his ethics to himself, and have given you something more real, more substantial, for his much tormented

and rather seedy offspring. But let us drop
the subject, and speak of your family. Your
poor mother and sister—I really feel very
sorry for them. You must know that we
always clung faithfully together during your
stay in Africa; and I may say that I spent
many a happy hour in that little summer-
house near the high road; and when my
Cousin Nicola came from the Residence, and I
from the military school, what a gay, delightful time that was with my sisters and with
your sister, Leonhard, in the meadows and
on the hay waggons. Yes, that was a
pleasant life indeed; and in those days there
was really no need for thrusting the *code
moral* under one's nose; and I tell you,
Hagebucher, I don't think there is another
man so well fitted for rational farming as
myself and—pon my word, I will prove it
yet to the world, as well as to the old man!
Devil take me if I don't do it, and that very
shortly too."

"Are you, then, so very tired of your present profession, lieutenant?"

"*Tired!* This word by no means comes up to my feelings. Tired, indeed! No natural philosopher has ever meditated more profoundly on a name for a new kind of insect, than I on a new expression for my present state of mind. My sole hope in this perplexity is your Coptic professor. If *he* does not find a word for it in some Egyptian vault or pyramid, or a suitable expression in cuneiform writing or hieroglyphics, I am done for, and shall give up all idea of publicity and verbality, confining myself to mute repentance and silent contempt. Oh, do not laugh, my dear friend! If I were to go to Tumurkieland at this moment, and hold a lecture there, I am firmly convinced that the ladies in that country would appreciate my sufferings fully as much as the sweet girls, agreeable widows, and lovely wives here did justice to yours."

"That I'll believe!" laughed Hagebucher. "But, pray, in what do your troubles consist? You are young, healthy, and know very well how to get round your papa, without allowing an exaggerated delicacy of feeling to stand in your way."

"Oh, hang it!" exclaimed the deeply mortified young warrior. "That is the worst of it, that nobody will believe in the sufferings of a sub-lieutenant, and that those to whom he confides his sorrows will accompany his groans of despair by the ironical assurance that they believe every word, and only wonder how a man so heavily afflicted could have attained such an advanced age. How happy all these singing, fiddling, and strumming individuals are, who can ventilate their sorrows by help of their art! But what can I do? I can do absolutely nothing! No, and yet I know how to play whist and ombre; but these, to be sure, are both arts with which it is difficult to express what one suffers, and by which one rather lightens one's purse than one's heart. Oh, Lord, Hagebucher, so you know how low down a fellow can get?"

"I believe to have some experience in it," said the man from Tumurkieland; but Lieutenant Hugo von Bumsdorf dealt him a friendly blow on the chest, and cried—

"You? Pshaw! don't flatter yourself. What can you know about it? You will admit the utter vanity of this when I tell you that I, Hugo von Bumsdorf, Lieutenant in the 2nd Lancers, have times when I— when I actually am driven to meditate on the immortality of the soul."

"That is awful, to be sure!" said Leonhard, whilst the lieutenant continued—

"And yet that is not all. Just fancy that I even tried to discuss and solve the question with my comrades in the *café!* What do you say now?"

"Indeed I can only admit my presumption.

But what was the opinion of your comrades?"

"The opinion of my comrades? I really don't believe they have formed an opinion about it; that they even thought it worth while to reflect upon it. With a scornful laugh, they passed over my motion; so I left the gentlemen in the bright sunlight, amongst the *nymphae*, hunting for dragon-flies,* and other winged and wingless dainties, and, like a sick carp, sank back into my own bottomless depth."

"Most graphically described," laughed Hagebucher. "Have you never thought of fixing these strange and instructive moods on paper? Have you never tried to free yourself of them, pen in hand?"

"Paper? Moods? Pen in hand? Sir, I told you before that 'the spirit which swells this bosom cannot manifest itself outwardly.' Please to notice the quotation; it is not from

* In German, "Wasserjungfer," water-maid.

Paul de Kock, but from Goethe's ' Faust.'
Do not look at me so surprised ; I study
' Faust.' The book lies always open beside
my bed, and I gave strict orders to my
servant always to let it lie there. Yes, this
Doctor Faust ! It is scarcely creditable ; but
for all that, shockingly true, that I sometimes
feel strong points of affinity between us ; and
the dark foreboding has long developed into
a settled conviction that my sole salvation
lies in earnest activity, in building some
grand aqueduct ; besides, woman's ennobling
influence. Just now I devote myself entirely
to the study of drainage ; and, upon my
honour, I hope some day to achieve wonders
therewith on my native soil. Yes, here's my
hand upon it, and who knows whether the
moment when we shall perfectly understand
each other, and be united by still nearer ties,
is not close at hand ? Faith, Hagebucher, I
have always considered you a very good
fellow, and it would seriously grieve me

to believe that you thought otherwise of me."

"I take you to be a good and faithful friend—a kind and light-hearted fellow, and I trust that you will ever remain so. *Ha mon joie Crillon!* I also believe that some day we shall sit in the shade of the elder-trees near the Bumsdorf high road, in the company of the ladies, and talk with great pleasure of these days spent in the Residence. Under all circumstances I trust that we shall do our best; and to you, Bumsdorf, I cordially wish all success in your contemplated hydraulics and agriculture."

"Amen!" •said the lieutenant, and then added, "You have no idea what pains a man in my situation has to take, to have a little bit of fun. Of enjoyment and comfort, there is, of course, no question; and I know but one person who is still worse off, and that is my cousin, Nicola von Glimmern."

"Nicola!"

The African, who had already accompanied his visitor to the door, and at heart was not displeased that he at last wanted to go, now hastily interposed his person between the door and the lieutenant, and exclaimed—

"You really must stay a few minutes longer, and tell me a little about the lady whose name you have just pronounced. You know how much interest I take in her life; and, moreover, I came but lately from the cats'-mill and Mrs. Claudine. During my absence you, no doubt, have seen her daily. I should really be very much obliged to you if you were to tell me something about her life. I, too, may say, that perhaps the hour is not very far off when I shall claim all your strength, all your good-will, for this lady."

The lieutenant once more laid down his cap, and looking at the African with evident surprise, he replied—

"Tell me what is in the wind. What is walking about like a spectre on tiptoe? in

one word, Hagebucher, what is going on?
There is a rustling and whispering in the
higher as well as lower circles, as our gilt-
edged poets would say. There's a cloud
rising in our social sky, casting its shadow
over all the coxcombs and wiseacres, the
gossiping dowagers and old maids, of this
abominable nest. Everybody seems to smell
something, but does not well know what.
You, however, seem to have cast a look into
this Pandora's box. What is it, Hagebucher?
What is brewing over the head of my beloved
Cousin Glimmern? I pray you, that, if it is
at all possible, to give me the watchword.
I promise that I will sacrifice all for my
Cousin Nicola—my moustache, as well as my
head, if it be necessary. You hesitate?
Well, then, I will give you another proof of
my confidence by not urging you any further.
But one thing I claim as my right; you must
call me at the right hour."

"I thank you, my friend," said Leonhard,

very gravely. "I will call you at the right
moment. But now tell me how is Nicola
since——"

"Since you held your excellent lecture,
afterwards to vanish in so marvellous a
manner? Well, I'll lay you a wager that
you might put this question to ten thousand
sub-lieutenants, and would ever receive the
same answer—her ladyship is very well
indeed. She is an exceedingly entertaining
woman, who understands very well how to
find out the right sides of existence. At the
ball yesterday, she looked bewitching; and to-
morrow, at the ball, she will, no doubt, be
again the fairest of the fair, that is, amongst
the married ones. But I, Hagebucher, I
heave an angry sigh, and ask, 'What have
they made of her? and what has that
foolish woman allowed them to make of her?'
Poor girl! She and I always were the best
of friends, and at that time, when the whole
of Bumsdorf gave me up entirely as the most

irretrievable of sinners, she alone had the
pluck to laugh at the whole stock of relations,
bathed in tears and drowned in misery, and
to retain her staunch belief in the jewel of
my soul and my noble destination. This I
shall never forget; but, devil take me, if I go
any longer into her house to witness that
wretchedness. What did I say? *Must* I
not go and sit down by her side? In former
times the knights and stalwart young cousins
slew all sorts of dragons which threatened the
ladies; but nowadays that is all changed.
The knights come and sit by the ladies' sides,
to drive away care by talking nonsense to
them. Bumsdorf *à la recousse!* I go every
day to see the poor girl, and try to cheer her
up a bit. And the dragon, her lord and
master, I put up with for her sake, which
also proves the total change of things.
However, it is always a great relief when
he takes his hat and stick, and vomits fire
somewhere else than at home. He is a very

polite dragon, who knows the world, and who, by his Bengal-fire capacities, knows how to bring about the most wonderful effects of light, and that not only at court. Here, by the way, one might put the chickenological prize-question, ' Is it permissible for a cock to lay eggs out of which——' "

" Stop—enough of this! For Heaven's sake, let the baron alone ! " exclaimed Leonhard, interrupting the imaginative lieutenant, who replied—

" With all my heart! Only too willingly ! Let us drop that excellent basilisk, and that no less excellent Cochin China or Brahmaputra cock—his late papa. We, that is Nicola and I, often sat together during your absence, but nothing remarkable occurred. We talked of one thing and another, just as I now talk with you. We spoke of Bumsdorf, of Prospero—you know Prospero, don't you, Leonhard? When we have more leisure, I must tell you a good story, how I carried

him off secretly, three years ago, and how
the governor came in a rage to fetch him
back. We talked of the cats'-mill, and of
Mrs. Claudine, the bewitched lady in the
mill. What we talked about! Ay, that
is the misery; for when I remember how
jolly we used to be together in the olden
times, this makes the present look all the
worse. She still laughs as she used to, but
it is no longer the laugh of old. Sometimes
I think that if she were to cry a little, it
might be all the better for her. Ah, Hagebucher, psychology is not the science a man
like myself generally excels in; but, I tell
you, that is a soul which I thoroughly understand. She has defended herself as long as
she could, and at last she made an honourable
compromise. But what can a poor, ill-used
woman do, if the promised conditions are not
adhered to? She cannot run away, as you
did, Mr. Leonhard; neither can she disappear
and become a myth, so to say, like that fool

of a Victor Fehleysen, of whom there is still
many a tale told in the city. She cannot
vent her wickedness on the recruits or at
the gaming-table, as I do. She has ever to
stand there, arms grounded, and must listen
to all the rude and insulting speeches of her
commander-in-chief. And that man, the old
woman at court, and the abominable weather
we have had of late, are all as pitiless and
inexorable as fate; and it would be no wonder
if they should get the upper hand of my
proud, fair Cousin Nicola, at last. Sir, you
are the man for me, and have learnt to hold
your tongue under the equator, of which you
have but now given me a proof. I respect
this, and admire every man who knows how
to wait calmly for the right moment. I
cannot do that, and so I take the liberty of
stating here before you, that, if the spectre
which walks about in that house does not
very soon make its appearance in public, for
instance, at noon, during the parade, I, Hugo

von Bumsdorf, shall become very unpleasant
to my Cousin Glimmern, and it would give
me immense satisfaction, at some suitable
hour, to shake his vile soul from out his
sleek body. And now farewell, and remain
my friend. To-morrow there is a ball at
M. von Betzendorf's, where I shall not meet
you, I dare say, but where I will give your
kind regards to Nicola in some quiet corner.
Good-morning ! "

The African proved that his young friend
was right with regard to his being able to
keep a secret. He kept all that he might
have called out after his retreating guest, to
himself, and took himself and his feverish
restlessness to Professor Reihenschlager's, to
that pair of sweet eyes which the dreamy
tailor, Felix Täubrich, so much admired.
But Serena smiled and pouted in vain, and
in vain did the professor exhibit all the
results of his scientific labours during the
last months, as well as all the difficulties that

he had encountered during the same space
of time. Leonhard had an awful headache
in consequence of the lieutenant's visit. He
often pressed both his hands against his
throbbing temples, and the professor's Coptic
vocabulary would noways exclude all that
he had heard from his young friend.

"This won't do, Serena," said the professor, thoughtfully shaking his head, when
their African friend had taken leave of them.
"This really won't do, my child. What has
become of all steadiness of purpose, logical
thinking, and a thorough appreciation of all
that's needful? What a deplorable absence
of mind! What a sad decrease of all philosophical, mental capacities! Ah! Father
Jove, and all ye other immortal gods, I
beseech you to preserve this youth——"

"Forty, forty!" muttered Serena, thoughtfully bending over her sewing.

"In the full appreciation of my—his high
vocation! By the Eleusinian mysteries, why

else should you have rescued him from captivity amongst beings who are unacquainted with salt ; and who can mistake an elegantly shaped oar for a shovel ? "

" Ah why ? ah why ? " sighed Serena, *pianissimo*, adding aloud, " Papa, don't take it ill, but you become funnier every day."

Leonhard Hagebucher first paid a visit to the late grand-duke in bronze, on the promenade, and then went to Major Wildberg's house, partly to make known his return, and partly from other reasons. Just as much as he felt the wish to be alone, when he was with people, just so much did he long for society as soon as he was without it. In short, don't let us waste another word on a state of mind which almost everybody knows from his own personal, bitter experience.

The major's house was soon reached, but it was not quite as easy to get upstairs, for the entire red-cheeked progeny of the worthy strategist and good Mrs. Emma kept this blockaded under the superintendence of two nursery-maids, and, with loud cries of delight, clung to the arms, legs, and coat-tails of the African, like a swarm of bees.

"He has come back! Mamma, the man from the country of the black men has returned! Hurrah! Vivat! Papa, here we have got the uncle with the stories about the elephants and lions! He is back! Hurrah, king of the blacks! Tell us a story of the big monkey and the crocodile, and the black men who need not wash, because it won't help them any, and who need not dress, because they have no clothes, and whose boots you had to black, and whose coats you had to brush so long."

"Halloo! All this will come in time," cried Leonhard, shaking hands with Mrs. Emma across this tumult of children's heads and hands. And the major came out of his study, where he had been occupied with a plan of Fort Sumner, and for some time tried

in vain to hush his hopeful offspring, until
a dancing bear, accompanied by a monkey
and a man blowing on a bag-pipe, came to
his assistance; upon which the unruly gang
of course abandoned the story of the monkey
for the living wonder, and noisily rushed
downstairs and into the street.

"Did you ever hear or see anything like
it!" exclaimed the major, raising his spectacles.
"Welcome, Hagebucher! We already knew
of your return, and are heartily glad to see
you once more."

"Come in quickly, Mr. Hagebucher!"
exclaimed Mrs. von Wildberg. "It always
seems to me as if life were like an eel in my
hands. Here, come into my husband's study,
for which that noisy gang has still a little
respect left, so that we may hope to remain
undisturbed for a while."

So the African found himself once more in
the well-known, comfortable apartment, was
offered a cigar, and had the full permission

to say all that he felt. The latter he did—
that is, until he came to the dark, heavy
obstacle that had been cast across his path,
and which he could not surmount. From
the Wildbergs, also, he received kind and
sincere assurances of sympathy at the loss
he had sustained, and likewise heard many
a thing about Nicola's life, though hardly
anything that was new to him.

"She comes as usual," said Mrs. Emma;
"sometimes for a mere glimpse, just to get a
breath of fresh, healthy air, as she says; and
sometimes late in the evening, when the
Baron von Glimmern is playing cards at the
military club. She always likes best to be
in the nursery, and if the little ones are
already gone to bed, she rarely opens her
lips, but lets us talk. It is heartrending.
Just ask my husband whether he can stand
it much longer. As for myself, I feel as if
it would break my heart; and if I do not
soon write a somewhat strange letter to his

Excellency, I do not know what is to become
of my nerves."

"My wife is right, Hagebucher," said the
major. "It is indeed a sad piece of business;
but who is authorized to interfere, and what
would be the use of it?"

Once more the African fancied he saw
Lieutenant Kind's shadow on the wall, but
this had no longer anything terrifying for
him. On the contrary, as he pronounced the
old man's name in the depths of his soul, he
thereby seemed to derive some relief. After
having further ascertained that the major
was going to Mr. von Betzendorf's ball,
without his wife, he took up his hat and went
away.

CHAPTER IV.

MR. LEONHARD HAGEBUCHER had certainly
no reason for complaining of the monotony
of his life just at present. He would have
wronged Tumurkieland as well as the German
Fatherland, if he had compared the two in
this respect.

In Tumurkieland, it is generally very warm
in summer, and the only clouds that darken
the sun are clouds of locusts, which, however,
by darkening the radiant aster for a while,
do not, therefore, produce any cooling of the
atmosphere; which, moreover, they do not
at all intend. The clouds of locusts are followed by the rain-clouds of winter, for it
rains terribly in Tumurkieland, so that the

summer dwellings are turned into mud, and
everybody moves into winter quarters. The
different families go to live in more spacious
caverns in the rocks, whilst the bachelors and
single maidens hire some more modest crevice
from kind Mother Nature. The slaves also
have their own receptacles, which, though
rather damp and musty, nevertheless have
their charms when compared to a life in the
open air.

Mr. Leonhard Hagebucher knew all this,
and never dreamt of comparing these national
peculiarities with those of his native country.
Neither did he underrate the latter, compared
to the former, and that least, on the morning
following the day we have but just described.

It was a very restless morning, in which it
became evident what significance the African's
person had attained in the Residence during
his absence. It was truly marvellous how
many people were struck overnight by the
thought that this African stranger might be

used for many a profitable, pecuniary speculation. They had all heard of his return
from the country, and came all to welcome
him, and to drop a word by the way, on this
and that matter, which they recommended
either to his practical judgment, or to his
kind heart, but, above all, to his careful consideration. It was indeed incredible how
many different elements were to be found in
this rather insignificant place, which now all
took an interest in our African's existence, or
at least believed to have such.

There came an editor, who was not the
court-bookseller, and who, in spite of the
prohibition of the police, wanted to have
the lectures which had not been held, written
down, in order that he might get them
printed. There came a photographer, who
was most thoroughly convinced that a *carte
de visite* as well as a cabinet-picture of Mr.
Hagebucher had become an urgent necessity,
and might prove a brilliant speculation.

Several acquaintances from the café tried to
extend their intercourse with their "good
friend" to his private domicile. Then, there
appeared two gaunt ladies, who hoped to win
the "much tried" man, for the blessed exertions of the "home mission." Further, there
came a young man bent on finding a subject
for a modern epos, and who believed he had
found this theme in the African's adventures,
and whom Hagebucher, without the least
regard of the contemporary and future world,
plainly asked to leave him unmolested, adding
that in the present times, he considered it a
sign of a decided poetical capacity, if a man
could *not* write any verses. Political parties
likewise extended their feelers in Leonhard's
direction—in short, the morning was exciting
and interesting enough, but, unhappily, Leonhard remained callous, unsympathetic, and
sad, and only smiled once, when he reflected
during the flowery ebullitions of the young
poet, what would become of the world—that

is, *his* world in particular—if he were to marry, and, moreover, to marry Miss Serena Reihenschlager ?

This same thought he uttered aloud, when, towards dinner-time, the flood of visitors had at last abated, and he was left alone with the pasha. After having several times softly said, " Why should I ? " he finally pronounced the great words : " Why should I not ? " in a loud and distinct voice, and thereby brought a side-line of his second European psychological development to a very satisfactory conclusion. Only a *side-line*, however ; the principal still ran straight into the thickest darkness and confusion.

Four words sufficed to express all the conflicting emotions that had stirred in his heart, just as the most prosaic-looking stamped envelope may contain the most passionate outpouring of joy or sorrow, and, like an echo, Täubrich Pasha repeated—

" Ay, why not ? "

" What do you know about it, Täubrich ? "
cried Hagebucher, slightly nettled. " Are
you clever enough to interpret my sighs
aright ? "

" 'Tis a pair of sweet eyes," said the tailor,
his head drooping to the left. " There is no
other girl in town with such a good face."

" And there is no second ladies' tailor who
is such a strange fellow as you are, Felix !
By heaven, and why should I not ? But
now let us drop the subject for a while, and
have our dinner. Afterwards you may bolt
the door against anybody. Do you hear ? I
have to cast a look into the ' Sanchoniathon,'
as I promised the professor to do so."

" Sancho—Sanchoniathon ! " repeated the
tailor, raising his eyes to the ceiling. Such
a melodious name must keep what it promised ; and with the settled conviction that
his patron had chosen a suitable book for the
occasion, Täubrich walked on tiptoe to the
door, and drew the bolt.

After dinner, Hagebucher read in the Sanchoniathon, and Täubrich Pasha sewed a
button on his own dress-coat, for he had likewise promised to adorn M. von Betzendorf's
ball by his presence, and that, in a very official
position. We all know that he was a very
handy and serviceable man, and that no great
festivity could take place in the Residence
without his assistance.

"We only possess it in a Greek translation
of a certain Philo from Byblus; and there
are some who pretend that we no longer
possessed him at all," said Leonhard, dreamily
turning from his book; and then adding, "I
might now take her to my house, and my
dear old mother would receive her with open
arms! That is the great point of disagree-
ment amongst the scholars, whether she lived
in the days of Semiramis or Alexander the
Great, or whether she never existed. To me,
this is a matter of perfect indifference; as
she has certainly had opportunity enough in

her father's house to learn how to get on with odd people. His teachers are said to have been the Phœnician high priests, Hierombalus and Sarabalus. Oh, dear! I wonder whether she has also learnt in her father's house to refuse a fellow like me? Hierombalus and Sarabalus! I really think we should make a very nice and comfortable couple."

"That is my opinion also!" exclaimed Täubrich Pasha, hardly able to thread his needle, on account of his enthusiastic feelings.

"Ay, why not?" said Leonhard Hagebucher, ever more thoughtfully.

He flung the old Phœnician author on the table, jumped up, and paced up and down the room.

"I am no longer in the years when it is advisable to delay anything until to-morrow. This, however, might also be a reason for thinking well before acting; but—what do I

want? what can I yet attain in this crazy
European world? Indeed, I know the latter
well enough by this time, to be able to live
contentedly within the circle which I can
describe with the point of my stick. What
say you, Täubrich, if I were to put on my
coat about dusk, and go on my way to the
professor's? I should then probably find her
in the kitchen, beside the bright fire on the
hearth, and, to say the truth, she looks very
lovely in that light. I might first gaze a
few minutes with her into the flames, and
then, after we had both sufficiently collected
our thoughts, I might say, Serena, my dear,
I have come to a resolution. Will you listen
to the request of a somewhat odd, but for all
that very honest, fellow, for a few minutes?
And if she were then to shrug her shoulders,
and nod her little head, I might calmly
proceed. Serena, my dear, I have well thought
it over, and I would like to have you all to
myself, and your papa should not miss any of

his accustomed comforts in this change of
arrangements. I might then once more make
a digression into my past life, but not, I
trust, to the disadvantage of my prospects
for the future; and if at that moment my evil
genius were to let the kettle boil over, I am
firmly convinced that, looking a little rosier,
she would draw it back from the fire and
whisper, as she held the cover in her hand,
'Oh, Lord, Mr. Hagebuch—Leonhard.' By
this time the first kiss would certainly be
given, and we need only go upstairs to tell
the papa what had occurred."

It was really a pleasure to watch the pasha
at this moment, and during this description.
He had pulled out his thread as far as he
could, and thus held his arm motionless, his
mouth wide open, and his watery blue eyes
beaming with delight, and riveted on his
patron, who was entirely losing himself in
these delightful fancies that were starting out
from so dark a background.

And now he actually began to shed tears,
and exclaimed—

"Oh, Sidi, Sidi! you know best, and will
arrange everything as it is meet. All the
time, whilst you were away, I have racked
my brain to find out how it could best be
done, and now you come, you need only say,
'So it is,' and it is so. Sidi, you are on the
point of realizing my brightest dream, for
now you are going to do what I never could,
as fate did not permit it. You have stirred
the most melancholy, but also the sweetest
feelings of my heart, and I kiss the hem of
your garment for it. Yes, I also have been
'in Arcadia,' and was fitted to make a woman
happy. I often meditated over this at Mar
Saba, whilst repairing the old wardrobe of
my friends, the monks. I have always had a
strong inclination for building nests; but,
unfortunately, was too shy, in the Promised
Land as well as here, and but once I had the
opportunity of obtaining what I wished; but,

then, I did not want to. You must know
that this happened at Pera, where the old
widow of a shoemaker from Sirleberg was
bent upon taking me—not only as a country-
man of hers, but as a young and feeling man
—with her on her path through life. But she
was given to drinking; and, moreover, re-
pulsed me by various other physical and
immoral peculiarities. If it has its advantages
to be born with a tendency for the ideal, the
blue heaven, the stars, and the music of the
spheres, it also has its serious drawbacks in
life. At Pera, my married felicity came to
nought because my sense of smell was too
acute; and later, at Jerusalem, in my master's
house, nothing came of it, because my sight
was too sharp. But now, my greatest wish
will be realized in you, and she, the dear,
sweet, kind Fräulein has set her whole heart
on you, and you are very well-fitted for her
and the old gentleman, Sidi, and you will
take me with you wherever you pitch your

tent. Oh, Allah! It is most true that I
delight in the ideal; but now I clearly
see that it may be a great joy to live in
the world of reality, and not merely in a
dream."

"Dry your tears, and collect yourself,
Täubrich," said Hagebucher. "And I quite
agree with you that it is a great joy to live
in the world of reality, in spite of all its
sharp angles, wicked snares, and treacherous
wiles. Who was it who could have inspired
that wise fool Mahomed with the saying,
' All that intoxicates is forbidden'? Who is
to forbid poor, tortured mankind all that
intoxicates? As long as sorrow and sin and
death walk this earth, so long that, which
may produce a passing rapture, cannot be
forbidden! And now, my good Täubrich,
please to devote yourself entirely to your
dress-coat. I want to have one last consulta-
tion on the matter, and that, not with the
Sanchoniathon, but with Mrs. Claudine. In

a quarter of an hour I hope to be able to impart the result to you."

"God bless you, dear master!" sobbed the pasha; and the African filled his pipe, and stretched himself full length on the rickety sofa.

Whoever had seen him in this position would certainly never have guessed on what an exciting subject he was meditating, and what heart and soul-stirring problem he tried to solve, exerting all his mental capacities, and taking all *a priori*, as well as *a posteriori* experiences, which it had been his lot to witness, into consideration.

And the day advanced, and dusk was creeping on apace. The tailor was long ready with the getting up of his evening suit, and sat silent and immovable, the picture of breathless, though resigned, waiting; but the African did not seem to come any nearer to the solving of his problem. He, Leonhard Hagebucher, groaned aloud from time to time, occasionally changing his position and relighting his pipe; but, for all that, the light he was waiting for would not dawn upon him.

At one time he said—

"It seems to be dreadfully cold ⸱outside. Please to look after the stove, Täubrich."

Soon after, he unbuttoned his waistcoat, and passed his hand through his hair, like one very much oppressed with the heat. At five o'clock, he asked in doleful accents, what time it was; and a quarter of an hour later, the pasha, still more dolefully, said in despairing tones, from the depth of his disappointed soul—

"It is over! He won't do it! He will never get to do it!

The African breathed as softly and peacefully as a sleeping babe, in the dark, on his sofa, and things really looked as if he were not going to do it. So the surprise was all the greater when he dropped his pipe as it struck six, jumped up, and said, in his most commanding voice—

"Confound it, Täubrich, why don't you light the lamp? Are we a pair of owls, that we should spend all our lives in the dark? Where is my necktie? Where's my hat? That is a nice state of disorder! Quick, I say! Forward! *Bismillah!* I really am most cordially tired of this bachelor wilderness."

" Here, sir! Here ! " cried the tailor, jumping about like a frog, and trembling in every limb. The lamp was lighted; necktie and hat made their appearance; and the pasha was just about to give his patron a last finishing brush all over, when the latter pushed him back, and solemnly asked him—

" What date have we got? "

Täubrich named the day, and Hagebucher said—

" Not bad ! Not unfavourable." And then he recited—

" For ever and for ever, farewell, Cassius.
   If we do meet again, why we shall smile;
   If not——"

Without concluding the sentence, he softly closed the door after him.   The antics which Täubrich Pasha performed when he was gone, could not easily have been surpassed in grotesqueness, but they were perfectly well adapted to his momentary frame of mind.

CHAPTER V.

IN Tumurkieland people are likewise wont to marry. The young negro takes his negress, how and wherever he finds her, and the little darkies also follow, just as in Europe, in due time, and at fitting intervals. During his captivity in Abu Telfan, Mr. Leonhard Hagebucher had had ample experience with regard to love, happy and unhappy, in all phases and gradations, so that, in this respect, Europe had hardly anything novel to offer him; as that, which white people say and do under these circumstances, must be very similar in form and contents to the feelings and doings of the blacks.

When Mr. Leonhard Hagebucher descended

his staircase in the Kesselstrasse, he felt himself quite equal to this undertaking and all its consequences. The experiment appeared to him quite easy and smooth, and to be carried out without any particular exertions on his part.

This happy view of things, however, changed already considerably when he put his foot to the ground outside. Whether it was that the cold wintry air told on the African's nerves, or whether it was the sudden transition from the pleasant quiet *tête-à-tête* with the dreaming tailor to the unusually crowded streets, he felt a certain oppression which increased with every step.

"Courage! forward!" cried he, and once more tried to face the great hour with a smile; but this smile was very sickly, and breathing soon became rather difficult for him. Pulling his hat over his brow, as if the outer world had nothing to do with his present thoughts, he soon dashed it back and

stared about him, as if he could find comfort
in the things around him, of which he certainly stood in great need. After having
gone on still a little further, he already tried
to find some valid reason for delaying his
undertaking until the next day.

When he came to St. John's Square, he
really felt very bad; the perspiration broke
out on his forehead; he searched for his
pocket-handkerchief, and if he had not found
it in his breast-pocket, he would, beyond a
doubt, have considered this a plausible reason,
as well as a bad omen, and have returned
home. As it was there, as man, hero, lover,
nothing was left for him but to wipe away
the cold drops, and to continue his way to
meet his fate. If only some acquaintance
had met him, and had but hinted at a walk
round the town, a game of dominoes, or a
cigar in a quiet corner of some *café*, he would
gladly have linked his arm in that of his
friend, and postponed his proposal, and have

justified himself splendidly, to himself as well
as Täubrich Pasha.

But he met no one, except M. von Betzendorf's myrmidon, the same who had brought
him the superintendent's elegant note, pro-
hibiting his further lecturing. The man
politely raised his hand to his cap, and for
a moment Hagebucher looked at him with
a puzzled and thoughtful air; then, putting
his hand into his pocket, he gave him a
florin, and exclaimed—

"No; now I'll do it all the more certainly!
My good friend, I hope you won't fancy that
I should consider you an *omen nefastum*—a
sign of negation from the gods?"

"I don't fancy anything; but I thank you,
Mr. Hagebucher," said the man of public
safety, winking his eye at Hagebucher, as
he stealthily dropped the coin into his pocket.
"That is a species of coin which one doesn't
often come across," added he, with a shake
of his head, when Hagebucher had stepped

out of the radius of the gas-lamp, under
which this meeting had taken place.

So deceitful is fate! But rarely it puts
other obstacles in a man's way than such as
will tempt him to press forward to the point
where his evil genius wants to have him;
and I will by no means pretend that it were
much given to placing some pleasure, or
reward, at the end of man's path, like a
mother teaching her child to walk.

"Now I'll do it all the sooner," repeated
Leonhard, quickening his steps; and now
he would not have allowed himself to be
detained by a forgotten pocket-handkerchief,
or any chance meeting with some good friend.
One more corner to turn, and the professor's
house came in view. There it stood! No
evil wizard, from the interior part of Africa,
had rubbed Alladin's magic lamp to spite
Hagebucher, and had transplanted it by help
of the genii of the lamp, with its pretty,
clever, silver-voiced inhabitant, into the

middle of Tartary. Everything was in its right place, even the words over the entrance: *Introite hospites!*

The snow had been swept from before the hospitable gate, and heaped up on both sides. The lamplight from the professor's study cast a comfortable and tempting glow out into the night. A slender crescent moon stood over the white roof, the smoke was curling upward from Serena's chimney, and the silver moon seemed to smile at the African through this luck-foreboding cloudlet. Leonhard stopped one moment to look at the professor's window, the moon, the chimney, and the dark tree-tops in the garden. It was certainly another sort of hesitation than that which but lately had made him loiter before the cats'-mill, but, by Allah! there could be no question of a careless and indifferent stare to-day either. Serena Reihenschlager was surely in the kitchen, whither the African knew well how to find his way.

The full opportunity was now given him, after his long adventurous and wearisome zigzagging career through the world, to round off his life into a snug and comfortable circle, from the centre of which he might thank the gods for having brought him to this happy resting-place at last.

And still no obstacle! Hagebucher, who had had so many a fall during his life, did not stumble over the threshold of the house, and in consequence did not hear any warning voice which might have whispered to him, 'A Roman would have turned back.' On the contrary, a very savoury smell of roast meat met his nostrils, and it would have been very ridiculous to take that as a warning sign. The kettle was hissing merrily in Serena's realm, and the bright flames cast reflected lights on the kitchen walls.

Not the smallest stumbling-block in the passage, not the least trip on the threshold of *this* gate. And now—it could not have been

different, for it was just as he had foretold
it!—she stood before the black hearth in all
her prettiness, musing, and lighted up by the
dancing flames, exactly like some love-lost
maiden in a picture, and her picturesque surroundings, from the shining kettles and pans,
to the fine white cat which purred around
her, all contributed towards completing this
picture. She wore a smart little apron, with
two pretty little pockets very well adapted
for quickly putting away keys, thimbles, or
love-letters, hiding them from the curious
gaze of the world. At this moment she had
not put away anything, though, but, on the
contrary, had taken out something, a crumpled
sheet of paper, which plainly showed that it
had often made its way in and out, and that,
during the considerable excitement of the
owner, who had conned over its contents
more than once.

And again she read it, and, strange to tell,
she allowed the kettle, which Mr. Hagebucher

had so graphically described but a short while ago, to boil over already at this moment; but she did not pull it away from the fire, nor lift the cover. She read as a young author who reads his first proof-sheets; she read like an old jail-bird devouring the receipt which brings him an unexpected release from prison; nay, she even read like a young girl reading her first love-letter, or, like the girl's mother, when it fell first into her hands, that is, when she intercepted love's messenger and did not feel bound to respect the letter-privacy, which the state has guaranteed.

She read, and indeed her face was even rosier than those two imaginative people, Mr. Leonhard Hagebucher from the Mountains of the Moon, and Mr. Felix Täubrich, called Täubrich Pasha, from Jerusalem, had fancied. She read, and when Mr. Leonhard Hage-bucher could not restrain himself any longer, and announced his anxious, frightened presence, by an embarrassed cough, she uttered the little scream which had occurred in the programme, and exclaimed—

"Oh, Lord, Mr. Hagebucher!" The "My dear Leonhard" she did not say, but who will cavil at a word in such a moment?

What could the African do but prefer the question, whether he was in the way? and how could Miss Serena Reihenschlager reply otherwise than with, "Oh, dear, no; please to come in, Mr. Hagebucher?" If she had said, "Have you come again? Must you ever come at the wrong moment?" this would not at all have been according to the programme.

And still no obstacle! She quickly hid the little note in her pocket, and turning with redoubled zeal to her pot, she rescued its contents as far as that could still be done, and very soon recovering her customary self-possession, she lifted a very happy and smiling face to her visitor, and said—

"Good-evening, my dear Mr. Hagebucher."

"Good-evening, Miss Serena," said Leonhard, likewise smiling, and telling himself in confidence that it had been very superfluous, nay, confoundedly foolish, to have been so frightened at the prospect of this delightful moment. He felt so secure, so safe from all troubles, all terrors and vexations; a warm glow suffused his soul as well as his body, and the German cold, to which he had not yet grown accustomed after his long stay under the equator, no longer benumbing his muscles and sinews.

"Papa is in his room. If you will go up, I will presently follow, Mr. Leonhard," said Miss Serena.

"*Very* soon?" said Hagebucher, softly and tenderly.

"Certainly. As soon as the maid has returned from the well."

"Ah, Miss Serena, please to let me sit down here on the bench for a few minutes," entreated Hagebucher, divided between fear

of the water-fetching maid-servant and the
Coptic papa, both of whom he did not at all
require just now. " Only one short minute,
Serena. It is bitterly cold outside, especially
for such a chilly mortal as I am," added he,
shivering with delight; and with kind concern, the Fräulein placed a footstool beside the
glowing hearth, on which she put another
piece of wood, to increase the light and
warmth.

Not a trace of an obstacle! There he sat
beside the hearth, and she stood before him
with her right hand in the pocket into which
she had put the crumpled letter. There was
nothing in all the world to prevent his speaking out openly and freely, and unburdening
his heart, as millions had done before him,
happily arriving at the goal of their wishes.

" Ah, Miss Serena," he began, and really
gazed wistfully, as he had foretold, into the
dancing flames.

" Ah, Mr. Hagebucher!" sighed the

Fräulein without drawing her hand from out
her pocket, and then he made an effort like
one about to jump over a ditch, closed his
eyes, clenched his hands, and—took the leap.

"Serena, dear," he began again, and now
that he had once started, everything promised
to go on swimmingly. "Serena, I—we—I
have now thought it over quite long enough,
and head and heart won't bear it any longer.
You also have had full opportunity of knowing me, and I hope that you don't consider
me altogether a bad character, and your papa
—but what business is it of his? Oh, Serena!
my dear girl, I ask for nothing more in all
the world, if I have but you! Give me your
hand, Serena, and tell me quite frankly
whether you will be my wife? You—I—
we, Täubrich—I should so like to have you
all for myself, and your papa should not miss
anything—we would—we might——"

Indeed, what could and might they not
have done, if Miss Serena Reihenschlager had

not retreated several steps with a second and much louder cry of terror and surprise, stretching out both her hands beseechingly.

"Oh, heavens, Mr. Hagebucher! So you did mean it, after all? Oh, dear, dear! And that this should have happened just to-day!"

"I really do love you very heartily, Serena," continued Hagebucher. "The wanting youth I will try to make up by additional amiability. I am not a bad-tempered man, and I trust that we might make a very comfortable and peaceful household. My mother would be delighted; and as to your papa, I firmly believe that he would be glad to bind me with such close ties to the Coptic grammar."

"Oh, Lord! oh, Lord! that I am ready to believe; but it is all so dreadful; and the servant will come back presently. What shall I say—what shall I do? Dear Mr. Hagebucher, *he* has written to me just to-day. I got the letter this very morning, and he

excuses himself so much. In three days he
will come himself. All is settled, and there
is no longer any obstacle, and papa upstairs
knows everything."

"*Who* writes? What writes who?" cried
Hagebucher, utterly confounded, with wide
open eyes, and feeling like one who has un-
expectedly fallen into a morass.

"Ferdinand! Who else but my Ferdinand," sobbed the Fräulein. "Here I have
got his letter, and he was in the house before
you, and helped papa with the dictionary and
the grammar, just as you did. And papa
sent him away, which was very wrong
indeed; and so he went into the wide world,
to Hamburg and Edinburgh, and at last to
Geneva, where he became teacher of modern
languages. Oh, you don't know what hard-
ships he went through; and now he has
founded a school, together with a friend of
his, and he asks my pardon for not having
written so long, and the day after to-morrow

he comes himself, and papa knows all, and begins to see that he cannot prevent it any longer. He is now my own Ferdinand; and so, dearest Mr. Hagebucher, what more shall I say?"

"No, I don't think that anything is left for me to hear," muttered the man from the Mountains of the Moon, afterwards repeating the words, "He was in the house before me, and helped your papa with the grammar and the dictionary." Then, after a short pause, he added—

"So I have once more come too late! Oh, Täubrich, Täubrich Pasha!" and then he looked up and saw that the poor child no longer hid her hands in her pockets, but that she held her apron to her eyes, and was sobbing out her terror and grief behind it. Gently seizing her little trembling hands, he drew the curtain from her crimson face, and said—

"Dear Fräulein, if *you* will not speak to

your papa of this silly affair, *I* will most
certainly not do so ; and as to this pleasant—
this happy event, I offer my best congratulations to you and Mr. Ferdinand."

Serena had once more covered her face
with the apron, and could only express her
thanks for his kind wishes by a hasty, con-
vulsive nodding of her little head. As Mr.
Leonhard Hagebucher had no longer any
business in Professor Reihenschlager's kitchen,
he left it on tiptoe. Stepping out into the
dark passage, he hesitated a few moments
before ascending the staircase. Had he not
better go home and give a good thrashing to
poor Täubrich Pasha, to teach him never
again to be so thoughtless as to help a man
in committing a piece of folly, by all too vi-
vidly sharing his wishes and projects ? No,
an educated man does not try to rid himself
of such an irritability of the nerves in that
manner. An educated man does not go
home under such circumstances to whip

another man, just as little as he will throw
himself into the water or blow his brains out.
Leonhard Hagebucher went up to Professor
Reihenschlager. If we cast another look into
Serena Reihenschlager's kitchen, we shall find
her once more busily occupied with her pots
and pans. A faint smile is playing around
the young lady's lips, and the discord in her
soul seems to be entirely done away with.

CHAPTER VI.

THE man from the Mountains of the Moon
knocked at the door of the man whom he had
selected to be his father-in-law, listened, and,
believing to hear a deep sigh, he entered,
without waiting for the necessary permission.
He might in all probability have long waited
for this. The professor's pipe was gone out,
and with it, the professor himself seemed to
be quite extinguished. How deceitful ap-
pearances are apt to be! What a comfortable
light the lamp from the study had cast into
the wintry, snowy landscape outside, and
what melancholy and depression, what weari-
ness of body and mind, did it shine upon!

Amidst all his books sat the father-in-law
of that excellent tutor, Mr. Ferdinand Zwichmüller, utterly bowed down, and staring at
the wall, as King Belshazzar, with whose
non-Scriptural history he had but lately been
unsuspiciously occupied; never guessing what
mischief the postman had carried into his
house.

On what rocky wall, on what obelisk, in
what mausoleum was there to be found, in
hieroglyphics or cuneiform letters, the words
of consolation, telling him how his utterly
broken up and unhinged life might again be
repaired?

"Where? Where?" cried the professor;
and, like another Ophelia, he gave vent to
his utter helplessness and bewilderment in
verses, which proved that the most touching
and simple poetry of his early youth was
awakened in his muddled brain, as if he had
been under the influence of chloroform.

"That is a pleasant surprise!" muttered

he. "By the thousand-breasted Iris, what is now to become of me?

> "'The names of nations, men and streams,
> The winds and months are masculine.'

All the materials for an orderly life, a quiet old age, gone to the dogs!

> "'But women, trees, islands and towns,
> In Latin are feminine nouns.'

And, old fool that I was, I thought it was all over, and boasted of my slyness and circumspection!

> "'*Commune* stands for both, you see;
> It can both male and female be.'

Yes, it *is* common, Ferdinand Zwichmüller! Ah, what cuckoo have I hatched out in my own nest! And how consummately that child has acted her part! Ah, what shall I do, what shall I do!

> "'That which can never be declined,
> Must as a *neutrum* be defined,'"

said Leonhard Hagebucher. "I really believe

that nothing is left for you but to take the matter as such."

The professor rose quickly, and came to meet the African with open arms.

"Do you already know it? Has she sung out her happiness to you? Hagebucher, don't you leave me! Stay with me! Yes, that is the only true bosom that has been left me of the thousand breasts of our common mother. What do you say to this abominable affair?"

"I offer my best congratulations," said Hagebucher, as gaily as circumstances permitted; "and I really do not see any plausible reason for despair."

"You don't? Well, then, I humbly thank you, my friend. It is indeed strange; it is one of the most wonderful things in this world, that even the wisest and most reasonable, the most prosaic and matter-of-fact, cannot leave marriage alone. Ay, there is no reason for despair, I grant you; but, as a sentient being, as an unprejudiced observer of human folly, I am very much annoyed."

"If Mr. Zwichmüller is otherwise a decent man—— "

"A decent man! I only wish that you knew him personally!"

"This would indeed give me special delight, particularly at the present moment," muttered the African.

"I wish you knew him as I know him! Such an excellent youth, and first-rate mathematician will not easily be met with, in this earthly vale of tears. He is much too good for me; and as to his exterior, there is nothing to object to whatever. He is so prosaic, so reasonable—ah, Hagebucher, there he was wont to sit in your chair; and then he used to let his underlip droop, just as you are doing this very moment, which makes me think that you also do not look as you are wont to do. Well, I thank you once more for your kind sympathy, for I trust that

from it springs your look of dissatisfaction.
What was I about to say? Ay, to be sure,
his underlip often hung ·down. Indeed, he
had to be handled very softly, for one could
never be sure not to have hurt his feelings
quite unawares. The young man has got
rather weak nerves, and can resent the most
harmless observations for six weeks afterwards. But as for that, he is very well-
matched with my daughter, and they will,
no doubt, lead a very happy and congenial
life together."

"Lord, bless them both!" grunted Hagebucher.

"As father and father-in-law I suppose it
is my duty to wish the same, but this can
only heighten my annoyance. For years he
sat there in your chair, and I have worked
for years at his education, in the sweat of my
brow; and I may say that in the pauses
between our learned pursuits, I have often
entered most thoroughly upon the relations

between the two sexes. If he had been my
own son I could not have warned this
Ferdinand more anxiously, more tenderly.
If I am not mistaken I have already told you
how I, when these dangerous symptoms
began to show themselves, turned him
straightway out of the house, and that he
afterwards wrote to thank me for this correct
interference on my part. All this time we
kept up a continuous correspondence, and
that deep, deceitful man pretended that he
would never do anything without asking my
advice, and now he has done this! Here I
sat quietly, thinking of nothing, or, rather,
meditating profoundly over the η in $\pi\nu\omega$,
$\pi\nu\epsilon\nu\mu\alpha$, *snuf, snys, nas, sunt,* but never having
an inkling of that which was going to happen.
Suddenly the girl comes in like a whirlwind,
puts her hands over my eyes from behind,
laughs and cries, giggles and sobs, kisses me;
and when, utterly puzzled, I ask for the cause
of all this to-do, she pokes a letter under

my nose, which quickly sends all learned
meditation wool-gathering. What do you
think that rascal writes to me? He writes
of the keen sight of fatherly love, and
that his esteem and regard for me were
beyond expression, and so on; and that he
were quite able now to support a wife.
Hagebucher, Hagebucher, do you know what
a dunce is? I did not know it, but at that
moment the exact meaning of the word was
revealed to me. I sat there like a dunce,
and the girl stood before me and had nothing
else to do than to embrace me over and over
again, and to cry between her sobs, ' Yes,
papa, dear, dearest papa, it is so, it is really
so; and it is such an old story, and if you
were not my dear old silly papa, you would
not make such a face at it!' Now I put it to
you, Leonhard, what face was I to make?
If I recover from this blow within a fort-
night, I'll consider myself extremely lucky.
I. will not quarrel with the gods, but why

must this happen to me of all others ? Why
must the most sensible, the most reasonable
and hopeful young men become fools under
my very nose ? Is it because I've got a
pretty daughter ? Is that a reason ? *Habent
sua fata puellæ !* To be sure, they also have
their fates to fulfil ; but was it really necessary
for the embellishment and preservation of
that which Marcus Tullius Cicero calls the
dwelling of gods and men, *domus communis
deorum hominumque*, that my own flesh and
blood should pull down the roof over my head ?
Oh, Hagebucher, why were you not called
Zwichmüller, and why did not fate take that
other one to the Caffres and Hottentots ? for
I am sure that *you* would never have played
me such a trick ! Yes, you are my sole consolation. At this moment your presence comforts me, but in the next days, when that fool
from Geneva will have arrived to settle
everything with my daughter, it will be in-
valuable to me, and nothing could replace it."

"Professor!——" Hagebucher began, fetching a deep breath, like some one about to make a long speech, and who, having a great deal to say, is inwardly preparing that which is weighing on his mind. "Professor," said Hagebucher, with marked emphasis, in a deep voice that trembled with suppressed emotion, and then—then he broke off, fervently shook hands with Papa Reihenschlager, and, all but staggering, went out of the room.

When he had reached the staircase he continued his speech, that is, he condensed it and brought it to an end. The most awful curse of the Bagarra negroes did not suffice to express his feelings, and at the right moment he remembered a benediction of his friend Semibecco—*that* word he pronounced on the stairs, and that word did him good.

. Softly he went down, leaning on the bannisters and slinking past Serena's kitchen door without being heard. Opening the

house-door, he was startled by the loud tones
of the bell, and so he did not escape his fate
after all.

" You are not going, Mr. Hagebucher, are
you ? " said Serena's voice behind him, and
it sounded as clear as the house-bell; and,
moreover, so serene and merry, so free from
all trembling and hesitation, that it was a
pleasure to hear it, except for the African.

" Yes, I am going, Fräulein. Good-night.
Please to give my compliments to Mr. Ferdinand in your dreams."

And so he went.

When he stood once more in the street, he
tapped his forehead with the knuckle of his
right forefinger, and he fancied he heard a
hollower sound than usual. We will also
refrain from repeating the form of speech in
which he expressed the old wise saying,
" Know thyself ! " from the same reasons, which
prevented our repeating the favourite exclamation of his friend the ivory-dealer, Semi-

becco. That he thereby came very near the truth, can, unhappily, not be denied.

The town was filled with an unusual stir and bustle. Private and hired carriages were noisily rolling along, carrying the invited— the elect—to M. von Betzendorf's festivities. Through the brilliantly lighted show-windows of a glove-shop, Leonhard beheld Lieutenant Hugo von Bumsdorf in earnest discussion with the presiding goddess of the store, and hastily passed on, before the young warrior had completed his bargain.

Going home? With an involuntary shudder the African remembered that the Sanchonia-thon was still lying there on the table, and that the only society he could count on was that of the old Phœnician. What if he went for a chat to Lieutenant Kind? That was an idea, for that man would just suit his present mood. Nay, he suited it all *too* well, and, shudderingly, Hagebucher turned away from this expedient to get rid of his own thoughts. At length he found himself, hardly knowing how he had got there, in a *restaurant*, with a bottle of *Rüdesheimer* before him on the table, and with the bill of fare in his hand.

He ate well, and it was not unnatural that he ate much. He drank another bottle of *Rüdesheimer*. The chatting of the guests around him, the continual going and coming, the broad, stolid face of the landlord, the automaton-like movements of the waiters; yes, even the pictures, time-tables, and placards of agents, and above all, the ticking of the clock, had a soothing, narcotic influence on his nerves.

He seized a newspaper, laid it down, and again took it up. At the other end of the table an old-standing guest was stretching himself out and yawning; bitterly complaining of the dulness of this earthly existence in general, and that of the Residence in particular. His neighbour, infected by the yawn,

cordially agreed to this, and passed on the
yawn. Leonhard Hagebucher saw it go from
mouth to mouth, and dreamily reflected how
much power of resistance he could offer, if
this tendency should venture to assail him,
and whilst he reflected, he was conquered;
and now, in defiance of his present mood, he
broke out into a merry laugh, and this was
the first real refreshment which the fates
accorded to him that evening. The guests
looked wonderingly at the jovial fellow, and
many, no doubt, envied him his flow of
spirits, but he paid his bill, lighted another
cigar, and stepped out into the cold night,
just as it struck eleven.

There was nothing whatever remarkable
to strike him on his way. The streets were
still rather lively, and people laughed or
grumbled over the severe winter. His ear
did not catch one word which might have
caused him to start or listen. Neither the
streets nor the people therein gave any token

that something had just occurred in the town which would be an inexhaustible theme for conversations, discussions, attacks, and enmities, not only for weeks, but months to come; which would break up entire circles in society, scattering them in all directions, and stir alike the highest as well as lowest grades in this shut-off commonwealth, and which, carried away by verbal as well as printed communications, far beyond the narrow boundaries of the duchy, would subject the Residence as well as the entire realm to a vast deal of gossip.

"If I only found Täubrich at home," mused Hagebucher on his way. "I believe that if I could load off some of the disgrace on his shoulders, that I might look forward to the next sunrise with tolerable stoicism. But that worthy is at M. von Betzendorf's, stealthily enjoying very different delicacies from those that I would treat him to. By Jove, I do not feel above trying to put all the blame on him! Ah, it was pleasant at Abu Telfan; and in Cousin Wassertreter's back room, it was still pleasanter! It is strange to tell, but nevertheless true, even the Sanchoniathon may be a comfort under certain circumstances. I will go and read the Sanchoniathon. At the entrance of the Kesselstrasse, the full appreciation of the disappointment to which he had so gratuitously exposed himself, brought about a last paroxysm. He stamped his foot on the snow-covered ground, and exclaimed—

"That is the consequence, if one does not rely solely upon oneself. Would I ever have thought of putting my nose outside the door this evening, if it had not been for the persuasions of that abominable fool, that harebrained Täubrich? With the thermometer twenty degrees below zero! Indeed, I will not make a scapegoat of the pasha; but the sentimental, love-yearning minute would have passed by, but for him, and the next

morning would have brought a clearer insight
into matters.   Ferdinand!   It is too absurd!
. . . Ferdinand   Zwichmüller!   Zwich —
müller! and if one could at least pretend that
the child was doing wrong, and not knowing
what was best for her!   But she knew right
well to whom she had best give her heart;
and I really should like to know what would
give a fellow the mere shadow of a right to
complain?"

By this time he had reached his house-
door; and, seizing the knob, he gave vent to
the remainder of his feelings in strange
sounds and growls from Abu Telfan, which
was hardly a good sign for Täubrich Pasha.
As he mounted the stairs, however, a milder
frame of mind got the upper hand, and he
again expressed himself in German—

"I cannot haul him over the coals, for I
have not got him; but just because I have
not got him, I will give him a speech—a
very fine speech.   Ah, I have spoken to the

winds more than once in my life, and not always with so much of a reason. And, Täubrich, I will not allow you to interrupt me. Please to make a note of that. Bismillah, the opportunity for unbosoming oneself does not present itself so often as the world is apt to imagine."

With these words he entered his apartment, firmly convinced that he knew what he must say; but the aspect which met his view riveted him for some time to the threshold, and, by degrees, turned all the ire which his soul had yet retained into a gentler emotion. The curtains were let down, and the floor was strewn all over with fine white sand. In the centre stood the table, covered with a white cloth; and in a tumbler, beside the brightly-burning lamp, stood a nosegay, as fine as any gardener would give at this time of the year to a good friend who was not exactly flush of money. Before the bouquet lay a large sheet of white letter-paper, on which was written in large characters—

I CONGRATULATE!

and below, the signature, Felix Täubrich," with the sly observation, "in his absence."

Leonhard Hagebucher could not wipe a tear from his eye, for the simple reason that there was none there; but he must have been more hard-hearted than the worst of the Bagarra negroes, if he could have brought the least bit of resentment to this festive table. Smiling, and shaking his head, with his hat on, he stood before this altar of the most genuine affection, and fancied what dances and antics the poor, kind fellow, the dreaming tailor, Felix Täubrich, called Täubrich Pasha, had executed before this sheet of paper, before he set out on his way to M. von Betzendorf, his heart filled with the fairest hopes and dreams. And now the tears had all but come when he thought in what a miserable world of fools, this genuine, true fool—this fool, so pleasant in the sight of the godhead, this altogether foolish Täubrich Pasha from Jerusalem—was now standing behind the chairs in the capacity of waiter.

Then, he did make his speech, holding the sheet, with the congratulation in his hand, and directing his words straight at the pasha, occasionally turning to the table, and not omitting the necessary gesticulations.

"You wish me joy, Täubrich, and I accept the kind wish with my best thanks. She won't have me, and she has her own reasons for this, which we are bound to respect. We were both mistaken, Täubrich Pasha ; but the gods have given a great strength into the mouths of children. I went out with a foolish hope, and I return with a heaped-up measure of newly-gained wisdom. I thank you most heartily for your well-meant congratulations, which have come at a most suitable time and occasion. We ever remain

children; and, no matter how wise we grow,
we always retain the desire to play with
sharp knives and pointed scissors. Now, let
me argue a little, as you are the only man in
this nest with whom one can sensibly discuss
this matter. You and I know by this time
that one is not always lucky enough to be
able to choose one's own public. What in-
duced me to make this experiment, Täubrich,
and what did I expect to gain thereby? Rest
—contentment'—happiness? I, the man
from Tumurkieland? I, the man from
Dshebel al Komri, the Mountains of the
Moon? You may well shake your head,
Täubrich Pasha. To be sure, in the mysterious rustling above your foolish head, there
is a melody in which all that is delightful for
body and soul finds its expression; but, alas!
over my head there is no rustling, neither of
the palms of the Orient, nor of the beeches
and lindens of my home. An empty, dark
space extends from east to west, from midday

to midnight; and it was sacrilege, it was a
downright cruel thing to say to a poor, child-
like creature, Come and sit down in the
shadow of my trees! That's what I have
done, Täubrich; and I did it at a moment
when I longed for a cloud,—and were it the
darkest of storm-clouds, to interpose itself
between this pitiless bright sun and my poor
head. Do not shake your head, Täubrich!
That was all the shade I had to offer the poor
child, and which I did offer to her. Yes, I
found it too hot and too dull in this scorching
sun, under this bright, blue sky, and I forgot
the Mountains of the Moon and my citizen's
right at Abu Telfan, my grey hairs, and my
long years; and because I, in spite of my
forty years, still feel younger than this gay
world round about me, I thought that I had
the same pretensions to happiness as other
people, and so I put the momentous question
to the Fräulein. I congratulate! Yes, congratulate, Täubrich! yourself, the Fräulein,

and me. But, above all, yourself, for I had
a strong inclination during my walk home to
make a terrible, a cruel example of you, on
account of your tempting insinuations, and—
here I stand, smelling your flowers, and observe—— "

What the man from Tumurkieland observed
remained a secret to posterity. Somebody
knocked at the gate below, then stumbled on
the staircase, and was now knocking at the
door. The thought shot through the African's
brain that the professor had, after all, heard
from his daughter all that was necessary or
unnecessary, and, prompted by his feelings,
had come, even at this late hour, to evince
his deep gratitude. But instead of the latter,
somebody else entered, shown up by his
landlady, who had been rudely awakened
from her slumber; and this person, whom
Hagebucher was not at all expecting to see,
was no other than Major Wildberg.

CHAPTER VII.

Who ever heard the explosion of the mine
which blew him up into the air? The crash
came, perhaps, while those it concerned were
thinking over very different things than the
threatening, ominous digging and working in
the depths below their feet. Their thoughts
had lost themselves in the distance; it is so
wearisome, so dull, always to stand on the
same place, shouldering the gun, and listening
to that which is going on below! Though
a sevenfold armour of steel may clasp our
breast, our soul will wander forth, and we
cannot hinder it. Beyond the furthest battle-
ments and ditches, it strolls about amongst
the fields, gathering poppies and corn-flowers

in the barley-fields; or, maybe, some lovely
rose peeping over a garden hedge, or a
sweet forget-me-not growing beside the murmuring brook; and in the midst of war, this
soul of ours is dreaming of the most profound
peace. And whilst it saunters along, culling
flowers and rejoicing over golden butterflies,
in the abyss below, a wild, grim, mocking
face is bending over a hardly visible spark,
and blows on it until it kindles into a flame.
A red glow passes over the face, lighting up
the mocking smile of the enemy. The match
touches the tinder—*tempus fuit!* Time was;
—there is no longer any time to call back
the erring soul, straying amongst the green
fields, from dwelling on the past or the future,
from repentance or hope—there is not even
time for half the Lord's Prayer, or any invo-
cation to the powers above.

To be sure, after such disastrous fireworks,
there are generally some people who escape
with sound limbs, almost unhurt, and are

merely a little confused, when, after being
picked up from amidst the shattered beams,
walls, and comrades, they are questioned
about the sensations they experienced. Such
people are apt to stare about wildly, or rivet
their eyes on the place where they stood
before they were blown up, and—have nothing
to say. On the contrary, others had to tell
them of that which had happened. How the
earth had opened with a fearful crash; how
the fiery jet had flashed out high into the
air, and a black cloud, shaped like a fan, had
spread over the scene of disaster; and how
horrible the shower of blackened fragments,
stones, ashes, and bloody human limbs, had
been. In this situation our good friend
Leonhard Hagebucher found himself at the
present moment. He had gone up into the
air, and Major Wildberg, who from his
whist-table had had the best opportunity to
witness the frightful event, with hairs standing on end, and wildly staring eyes, had

now come to acquaint him with the necessary
details.

Major Wildberg made his appearance in
the African's room in full gala dress, but
certainly not with that calmness and self-
possession which befitted his costume. In
spite of the severe cold, he carried his cloak
on his arm, evidently not having allowed
himself the time to put it on, or even to
throw it over his shoulders. His uniform
was buttoned all awry over his white waistcoat, and if Lieutenant Hugo von Bumsdorf
had ever worn his scarf in public as his
superior officer now wore it, he would certainly have had time to meditate, in the
solitude of a week's confinement to his own
room, on the important difference between
right and left, front and back.

Hagebucher dropped the flowers of the
dreaming tailor and uttered an exclamation,
which, just because it was in itself meaning-
less, expressed everything — perfect know-

ledge, the greatest terror, and also the first
groping step into the future.

"Now! Now! Has it happened?"

"First let me recover my breath, dear
friend. This is awful! What a night! Do
you know what leads me hither—what news
I bring?"

The African nodded assent, and mechanic-
ally stretched out his hand for his hat. The
major dropped into the nearest chair, gasping,
and searched for his pocket-handkerchief to
dry his forehead.

"I come from the ball of the superintendent
of police. The ground has given way under
the very feet of the dancers. Have you not
heard the crash and the outcry? Nicola is
with my wife, and I've come here. What a
night! Gilmore is at this moment bom-
barding Fort Moultrie, near Charleston, with
five - hundred - pounders — one such shell,
twenty-five inches in diameter, has fallen
amongst us. If the sky had suddenly come

down, the consternation could not have been
greater. Of all those who were present,
there is not one who has retained the control
of his five senses, and M. von Betzendorf
perhaps least of all. Come along, Hagebucher. Counsel, help us! Cast everything
aside, hatred and anger, friendship and pity,
for we need a clear head and a strong hand
—nothing else! Come on quickly, for our
sole hope is that you will not allow anything
to confuse you; that you will stand erect and
unmoved in this fearful calamity."

This was all very well meant, and, moreover, very flattering, and was a very suitable
ending to the speech which the man from
Abu Telfan, but a few moments ago, had
addressed to the imaginary Täubrich; but
the quiet and composure of our friend was
by no means so sure. Now the hour had
come whose approach he had so much dreaded,
and, at the same time, so longed for, during
the feverish excitement of these last days.

Lieutenant Kind was doing his worst. *How* he did it was a matter of indifference, but who, that did not have his own power of salvation within him, could be saved by a stranger hand from this terrible fate?

"Where is Nicola?" asked Leonhard.

"I have already told you. She fled to our house, to my Emma, in company and under the protection of your servant, your fellow-lodger—the strange tailor and waiter, Täubrich—and I have run here, for she demands to see you. This is one of those cases in which one is inclined to call any one happy who is killed on the spot."

"There is but one path for her; she knows it, and she will take it," muttered Hagebucher; and then he firmly pressed his hat over his brow, like a man who knows that a gale awaits him outside, took the major's arm, and said—

"Now we will go to her. Not I, she— she stands erect. Don't you fear for this woman. Take my arm, my friend; in the street you will tell me what happened at M. von Betzendorf's."

They descended the rickety staircase, and stepped out into the Kesselstrasse, which slept peacefully, aware of nothing that had transpired. The Kesselstrasse had not the honour to know M. von Glimmern, and as to the superintendent of police, this excellent man only came into contact with it through his subalterns, and therefore its inhabitants were perfectly indifferent as to the disagreeable position into which the honourable man had got, through this *éclat* in his house. The Kesselstrasse had its own cares, troubles, and excitements, and it is hardly to be expected that it should rise from its straw mattress, for those people in another world.

The Kesselstrasse slept peacefully, but there were a good many streets which did not sleep. Many a carriage rolled past the major and his companion, and the light of the lanterns shone on pale, terrified faces.

"That was the *Tribunalrath* Igeler, with his daughters," said the major. "He sat beside me at the card-table when the lights went out, and the doors flew open, to let in the spectre. For God's sake, Hagebucher, how can you have any intercourse with such a ghastly personage as Täubrich Pasha?"

"Poor fellow! What has he to do with this dark story?" cried Leonhard.

"He? By Heavens! how could the spectre have come in without him? He led it by the hand, so to say, and leading it right up amongst us, introduced it to us."

"*He* led in Lieutenant Kind!"

"Lieutenant Kind? To be sure, the pensioned Lieutenant Kind of the *Straf-compagnie*. Have patience yet awhile; memory comes back by degrees. It is as if all were shrouded in a mist—just wait— yes, it was so! We were having a rubber of

whist, our host, M. von Glimmern, the
Tribunalrath, and I. Betzendorf sat at my
right side, the *Tribunalrath* at my left, and
M. von Glimmern sat opposite me. We sat
in a side-room, and Glimmern had his back
turned towards the door which led into the
ball-room, where the dancing was going on.
I am no great hand at whist, but I felt very
comfortable, for I love such gay music, such
a merry march, and am still able to take an
interest in the pleasures of the young people.
So I paid more attention to the couples
gliding past the door than to my cards, not
to my own advantage, and M. von Glimmern
had given vent to more than one warning look
and pointed allusion—but what can a man do
against his nature? I was thinking of the
years that are gone, and how my Emma was
a much pleasanter partner than this ironical
Excellency, and how well my Emma danced,
putting all other girls, even the proud beauty,
Nicola von Einstein, into the shade, with her

kind, sweet smile. And so I thought how it came that I am here and she at home, and I could not make up my mind which of us is most to blame, and so the *Tribunalrath* of course once more trumped my ace."

"And Glimmern? Glimmern?" impatiently cried Hagebucher.

"He spoke Greek like Cicero, or rather he smiled and gave utterance to his opinion in French. But, as I said before, I felt quite well and happy; in short, I was in the mood to take everything from the bright side, and not to think beyond the next hour."

"Where was Nicola?" inquired the African.

"We exchanged a few words together in the beginning of the evening, but as she had been at our house in the afternoon, we had not much to say to each other. Very soon afterwards I lost sight of her, and to tell the truth, I did not much look after her, for there were a great many guests; and it is a

peculiarity of mine that I find it very difficult
to distinguish one woman from another—my
Emma excepted—when they appear *en masse*,
and are dressed up."

In spite of his excitement, or perhaps for
this very reason, it struck the man from
Tumurkieland as curious, how lengthy and
prosy this long peace had made the younger
as well as the older officers of the German
confederation in all their accounts. He felt
almost tempted to impart this observation to
the major, but thinking that the time were
hardly suited to this, he refrained.

They had by this time arrived opposite the
house of the superintendent of police, and,
moved by the same feeling, they both stopped
and glanced up at the stately building. Some
of the lights were not yet extinguished, and
restless shadows flitted past the curtained
windows. Before the half-opened gate stood
a group of men in earnest conversation, and
again a carriage rolled past the corner, and
entered the *porte-cochère* of the building.

" That was the superintendent himself, and I can tell you from whence he comes. He was at the palace, to make his report and to receive the wishes and commands of their Highnesses with regard to this case. The poor man! He was very intimate with Glimmern, and one need not envy him his present duties. And what will to-morrow bring ? "

" What do the masses regard us ! " exclaimed Leonhard, almost roughly, as he dragged the worthy officer on. " This is like a field of battle after the fight. We will have nothing to do with the marauders and grave-diggers. And now tell me how Lieutenant Kind got into the ball-room."

" M. von Glimmern was dealing the cards for a new game, and I had requested your Täubrich to bring me a glass of water. I believe that another dance was just about to begin, when *he* stood in the doorway, and that Täubrich beside him, holding a salver in his trembling hands. He wore his uniform and his sabre, and I took him at first for some masked individual. To reach us, he had crossed the ball-room from one end to the other, and he had attracted considerable attention. Some of the young folks were laughing, and a few pretty girls' heads were peeping round the corner, and Mad. von Betzendorf followed at his heels, looking at him from top to toe with surprised eyes; but M. von Glimmern did not see him, as he sat with his back towards the door, dexterously dealing out the cards. The superintendent's attention was only roused by the observations of his wife, as well as the *Tribunalrath* and myself, but that worthy is so accustomed to see so many strange customers professionally, that he at first merely raised his eyebrows, slightly surprised. He was just about to rise, probably to prevent the strange visitor from creating any further disturbance; but just then, your Täubrich gasped out, ' Lieutenant

Kind!' and the lieutenant put his hand on
Baron von Glimmern's shoulder. I am rather
a nervous man, and observe many a trifling
thing when my attention is once roused, and
now I saw everything very accurately, and
can give you a full description. He put
his hand quite gently on his shoulder, as
if he wanted to use it for support, quite
calmly, which impressed one all the more
uncomfortably. M. von Glimmern, who
must not have heard Täubrich's announce-
ment, at first never looked round. He, no
doubt, believed that some acquaintance was
touching him, and, calmly smiling, he dealt
out the last card. When he did look round,
the smile vanished from his lips quickly
enough. He started, and bit his lip. 'I am
Lieutenant Kind!' said the lieutenant, and
he said it neither roughly nor threateningly.
'What is the meaning of this, sir? what do
you want with me?' asked the baron; but
the old man tapped his shoulder without

replying, and turned towards us, whilst the lady of the house looked around for one of the servants. By this time, Nicola stood between the red curtains of the door, just behind Lieutenant Kind, who, as I said before, had turned towards us, and said, in a low voice, like one who does not wish to attract attention, 'The gentlemen ought to be careful with whom they sit down to play. A white glove often hides a dirty hand, and many a false card falls on the table unperceived.' We had all jumped up, and M. von Glimmern had upset his chair. 'That is a madman; how has he come in?' exclaimed our hostess; but the old man said, 'No, madam, it is no madman; it is Lieutenant Kind, and he has a right to come here.' And then he rose to his full height, and cried, in a loud voice, 'I denounce the Baron Frederic von Glimmern, in his own company and amongst his friends, as a cheat and swindler! This suits me best, and I dare say the gentlemen present will also like it best so.'"

"How fiendish! How refinedly fiendish! Oh, vengeance is a great artist!" exclaimed Leonhard Hagebucher.

"It was the shell from the Blakely mortar!" cried the major. "It fell amongst us, and burst into a hundred and thirty fragments."

"In his company, before his friends!" muttered Hagebucher. "And Nicola? Nicola?"

"I see everything through a fiery mist. I see papers in the *Tribunalrath's* and M. von Betzendorf's hands, and a crowd of pale, terror-stricken faces, uniforms, bare shoulders and arms, gay feathers and flowers. The small room in which we sat has vanished, and I find myself in the ball-room, where the dancing has ceased. I am utterly bewildered, like one intoxicated; and now everything is hushed and motionless, and only a tall figure, a woman in a white dress, walks past me,

and through the room, and all make way
before her. I call out her name, Nicola!
Nicola! but she never turns back. I am on
the staircase, in the street, in utter darkness;
and soon after, under a glaring gaslight,
amongst a crowd of people, come to listen to
the music-band. There are girls, women,
and footmen. Some laugh and scream; others
stare at me vacantly; and, again, others stare
down the street. Then Count Laurenburg's
lackey, a decent fellow, who once belonged to
my company, steps up to me, saying, 'A
lady went by just now, if you are looking for
her, major!' He stammers out the words
like one who does not know whether he is
doing the right thing; and then he names
your servant, Täubrich. And now—I am
here; and Nicola Glimmern has gone to my
wife, leaning on the arm of that same Täubrich. There I found her; and then I ran to
your house, Hagebucher, for as soon as she
had sufficiently recovered from her mad walk

through the streets to speak, she impetu-
ously asked for you, sending Täubrich for
her maid, and me here to the Kesselstrasse.
And now I beg you to tell me how you are
going to help that unhappy woman in her
unutterable misery?"

Leonhard mournfully shook his head, and
then said—

"Her flight is not yet ended in her running
away from the ball-room. As she looks back,
she sees her pursuers following at her heels.
She has still a long way to make through the
night, and I am to take her to the spot where
she hopes to find rest. Oh, I have been a
leader of souls during—— "

He stopped short, and then muttered des-
pairingly—

"Oh, my God, how can I take her there
now? That which might have been her
sole hiding-place, now only increases the
confusion and intricacy. Wildberg—Mr.
van der Mook—but no, away, away, let us

hurry. I will tell you more about it at your house."

They hastened their steps, casting many a look into the lighted windows they passed, and naming the guests of M. von Betzendorf, who were also still up, in consequence of the unheard-of event, and were either pacing up and down, or sitting, like paralyzed, before their lamps.

The major told off the names, adding, with a groan, " What an awful affair! and what will be the end of it ?"

They walked faster and faster, but before they reached the major's house, somebody stepped into their way who was also entitled to have his say in the matter—Lieutenant Kind, of the *Strafcompagnie* at Wallenburg. They met under a gas-lamp, and had sufficient opportunity to mark the physical and mental state in which the man was. A fearful, most startling change had taken place in his whole being. The grim, taciturn old

man had become a raving maniac. He, who
for so many years had exercised a stern,
almost superhuman self-control, had, with
the first word which he cast into his hated
enemy's face, lost all moderation, all self-
possession.

With a hoarse, animal laugh, he stood
right in the way of the two men, and shaking
his fists and gnashing his teeth, he cried—

"There you are, gentlemen. I knew I
should meet you before sunrise! Hoho, that
is the fight for which I have waited all my
life, and kept arms and uniform clean and
bright. Heigho, Major Wildberg! We should
never have dreamt that it would be so brisk
and merry as this, during the long time of
our idle parades and vain military shows!
War! war! Thus it is meet, so must it be!"

"You are ill; and it is no wonder that you
have got the fever, Lieutenant Kind," said
Hagebucher. "Go home now and shut yourself up in your room. You have taken your

rights, so why do you now err about like a drunken man? You have had your revenge, and it was your right to strike down the guilty one; but now step out of our way, and do not prevent us from removing the ruins, under which the innocent also have been buried."

"Does the wind blow round that corner, my dear fellow?" whispered the lieutenant. "Out of your way? Have you also got as far as the others, who wail and lament because a man took his rights like a man? The dog is always called mad that runs against the silken stockings and under the velvet trains. I wish you joy, Mr. Hagebucher! Have you learnt as much as that since your return?"

"I have learnt much, old man, and I would rather have cut off my hand than have stopt you on your path; rather bitten off my tongue than said one word to detain you. But now let us continue our way."

"But I won't! With whom shall I rejoice and share my triumph? Why did you take Mr. van der Mook away from me? Go, and give me back Victor von Fehleysen! Curses on him for having left me to do this piece of work all alone!"

Major Wildberg staggered back when he heard this name, clutching Leonhard's arm; but the latter calmly said—

"Mr. Cornelius van der Mook has been given into other hands than ours. But even here, I will not hold you back, Lieutenant Kind. Go and seek him under the roof, near the hearth of his mother, and take him away from thence, to exult with you over this hour."

The old man stepped aside, once more laughing harshly.

"Be it so, ye delicate-minded people, with the soft skins and the tender feelings. I go alone, and shall claim my winnings for myself. But I will demand the entire stake.

Blood for blood, a life for a life. The cards
lie on the table, but all have played false like
Mr. Frederic von Glimmern, and they also
will not pay. That is their habit; and they
think that they can do as they please, because
they rule in this rats' nest; and they think
themselves great because they have twenty
square miles to lord it over. He belongs to
their class, and though he is nothing but a
mean scoundrel and thief, it would yet be
improper and disagreeable to deal out the
same justice to him as to the tagrag to whom
they show up their miserable, copper-coined
gilt magnificence, as the best and finest thing
which the world holds. Ha! I tell you the
time will come when the auctioneer will strike
the table with his hammer, and sell the entire
trash to the German people. Twelve pre-
sidents for a penny, and the thirteenth to
boot! Twelve generals for a penny, and the
thirteenth to boot! But never mind that,
and let those who live to see the hour bid

for the shame. I will be satisfied with him
for whom I paid a higher price than all this
rascality round about is worth. With my
honour, my happiness, and the life of my
children, I have paid for the article, and the
bargain holds good. By the Lord above, it
shall hold good, and I defy them to find a
flaw in the calculation. Ha, there's a flaw
in all their calculations, for they always count
only themselves, and forget the hands and
fists below, which may be lifted against them.
Here we are, the dead and I, and if they will
chain their dogs, we must hunt down the
criminal all the more relentlessly. Let him
fly, the false gambler, the bloody murderer;
but we shall see whether our bark and our
howls, and the fear of our fangs, will ever
be out of his ears or his heart."

It was impossible to put in a word in this
wild and angry speech, and still more impossible to stop the furious old man on his path.

"There the gentlemen stand and stare,"

cried Lieutenant Kind. "Ay, ay, I dare say
he has escaped by this time, and he will not
have lacked money for his journey. Cursed
be they who prevented me from putting my
knee on his breast and my fingers on his
throat before this! Why do the gentlemen
look at me so? He is gone, but the dead and
I will pursue him, and we shall reach him
and settle accounts with him in spite of all
this false, corrupted, hypocritical world!"

Once more Leonhard Hagebucher stretched
out his hands towards him, but now he broke
away from them, rushing along like a blood-
hound on the scent, to use his own simile.

Major Wildberg leaned against the lamp-
post and groaned out—

"How powerless one is, just when one
would like to have the strength of the gods!"

But the African exclaimed—

"If he spoke the truth—and I hardly doubt
it—I will remain an honest man, and wish
him a successful chase. And now come on,

major; we will send Mr. van der Mook after
him. God is God indeed, and darkness is
his servant and prophet, as well as light."

"Victor von Fehleysen! Is that the
truth?" cried Major Wildberg. "Is not that
one of the bubbles rising in the witches'
caldron of this night, which will burst again
like a bubble?"

"Mrs. Claudine's son has returned to his
mother, and is staying with her in the forgotten mill in the bewitched valley, whither
Nicola von Glimmern may fly to hide herself
and find rest."

"The unhappy woman," muttered the major,
whilst Leonhard Hagebucher shrugged his
shoulders without saying anything further,
until they reached Major Wildberg's dwelling, where some one was awaiting their
arrival with feverish impatience. For the
space of an hour Lieutenant Hugo von Bumsdorf had been walking up and down before
the house, biting his moustaches and tearing

his gloves, but not venturing to ring the bell
and enter the house. Now he came forward
with a bound to meet the two men, and exclaimed—

"Nicola! my cousin! my poor Nicola!
Oh, gentlemen, gentlemen, what shall I do?
What must I do? How can I help? I
must do something for her, if I am not to
go mad. Hagebucher, tell me what enemy
I must strike down? What answer shall I
give to my father when he asks me what
post I held this night?"

"You shall not murder anybody, my dear
Hugo," said Hagebucher. "Try to calm
yourself, and come with us. We shall indeed
need your help very much; and we will not
allow you much time for fruitless meditation."

"For this I will thank you on my knees,"
exclaimed the lieutenant, as all three entered
the house.

The major softly led his companions upstairs, first showed them into his own room,

and then went to apprize his Emma of their arrival. During his absence, Leonhard acquainted the lieutenant in a few words with the person, the history, and the present abode of Mr. van der Mook, thereby very much adding to the perplexity of the young warrior.

Now Wildberg came back on tiptoe, and said—

" You go in, Hagebucher ; you will find her in my wife's room. Hugo and I will await your return, and hear what you will then have to tell us."

The African went and knocked at the door of the best *Frau Majorin* * who ever gave the watchword and war-cry to the most honest and peace-loving major.

* In Germany a wife generally takes also the professional title of her husband.

CHAPTER VIII.

It cannot be said that the man from Tumurkieland felt himself exactly master of the
situation, when he stood listening before
Mrs. Emma's door, and yet he was obliged
to admit that he and Mrs. Claudine were the
only persons whose intercourse and words of
comfort would at all be acceptable to the
unhappy wife of Baron von Glimmern.   Here
were two people, around whom fate had, so
to say, drawn a circle, as if thus to solve a
problem, and out of millions, Nicola Glimmern
was now alone entitled to cross this dark
boundary-line, which separated the bustle and
stir of life from the most complete solitude of
those two forgotten ones.

The door was softly opened.

"God be thanked!" exclaimed Mrs. Emma, drawing the African into the chamber, and whispering, as she pointed with a trembling hand at her friend, "Look at her! Help her!"

In a brilliant court and ball toilette, with bare arms and shoulders, Nicola von Glimmern paced up and down the room, trailing her long silken train after her; and she was wondrously beautiful in her savage, mournful magnificence, and yet unspeakably sad to look at.

She did not weep. Her delicate lace pocket-handkerchief she had long torn into shreds; she laughed through her locked teeth, and thus she approached the African, took hold of his arm, and gasped out—

"What did she whisper? What did she say to you? Why does she not speak out loud and distinctly, as usual?"

"Nicola!" cried Mrs. Emma.

"They will all in future speak low, quite low, in my presence, and I shall have to accustom myself to that. Pardon me, dear, there will surely come a time when I shall no longer stupidly ask after what is a matter of course. Good-evening, my dear friend. I hope that you were not roused from your slumbers on my account. It is rather cold here, and the sunshine under the palm trees must surely have spoilt you a little. Besides, it is rather late, and he who can sleep should do so, and we would herewith proclaim that it is forbidden, under pain of death, to cry out 'fire' at the door of all sleepers, before their own roof is in flames."

"I was wide awake when I heard of the fire in my neighbour's house," replied Hagebucher, in the tone of a doctor telling the town news at a sick bed, who well knows what he is about. "I was quite lively and wide awake, and there was no need for rubbing my eyes. I looked into a

basket, like a man on a guillotine, into an
empty basket,* which a very amiable young
lady had placed before me, after I had expressed my intention of making her my wife
and being happy the livelong day, or rather
the whole long life, together. But, as I said,
she thanked me politely, telling me that she
was otherwise provided for; and so, you see,
it was no wonder that I heard this alarm of
fire."

At another time Mrs. Emma would have
lifted her hands above her head with surprise
at this news, but at the present moment she
contented herself with naming that young
lady, and looking at Nicola.

But the latter pushed away Leonhard's
hand, and said—

"I hear many words, but it is so difficult
for me to attach any meaning to them.
Somebody spoke of marrying and being

* "To receive a basket," means to be refused by a
lady, in Germany.

happy, of an alarm of fire, and that basket
before the guillotine. Just wait a moment,
and I'll remember the phrase. *Cracher au
panier*, the ladies who looked on at the gay
comedy, knitting in hand, used to call it.
You should not marry, Hagebucher, without
asking my advice. I am a wise woman, and
might call up many a witness to this fact,
if I did not dread the loud voices of people
so much.

"We once went away together from the
cats'-mill," Hagebucher said, quietly; "that
is, you rode Prospero, and I ran beside you
on the high road, and then we talked a good
deal of the days that might come. You
carried Mrs. Claudine's black bread in your
bosom, and before we parted on the height,
past Fliegenhausen, we spoke of a realm of
liberty, calmness, and proud resignation,
whose citizenship we believed to possess. We
also spoke of how we might meet again,
perhaps in some evil, death-threatening hour.

Then we were to remind each other of that bright realm, and that citizenship, and those clear, peaceful eyes in the mill, were to keep watch over us. Now, Nicola, we will keep true to ourselves, and prove to the world what we promised. Are you no longer the Nicola of old, who asserted, with a laugh, that she would remain free in all chains? Look up, and look into your own heart. In our realm, one clings most to victory, when our enemies are exulting most and shouting triumph. Oh, recollect what you were, and what you are, Nicola Einstein!"

"That is the question, to be sure, but I cannot remember. You talk of dreams which I dreamed a hundred years ago, as if they were real; but all this has no meaning for me. What am I? A poor, trodden-down woman; no heroine who, riding on a white palfrey through the woods on a summer evening, is taking the witchery and loveliness of nature for her own courage, her own

thoughts and feelings! When we first met,
I was an old maid, who, by some magic, had
retained the last illusions of youth;—now,
I am a weary old woman, whose only realm
is based on everyday things, and who sinks
with them, never to rise again. Do not
shake your head at me, for you know, as
well as other people, that that life which
deals so pleasantly with us to-day, is, after
all, the only true and real life. You are a
sensible woman, Emma, and have always told
me so. Now, please to convince this good
man, and let him pay you with sighs and
tears. Now we have got as far as was
necessary, in order to be of use to the public.
The whole matter is very instructive.
Eternal justice steps out from behind the
scenes just at the right moment, and in the
right place, and gives everybody his due,
according to his deserts. Oh, it is a very
sweet and refreshing thought in all this
misery, that, after all, one is nothing but

an illustration in the great A B C book of the world, and that those serve her best, who most expose their personality in the pillory to her looks, gibes, and stone-throws. Ah, my head, my poor head! Who would have thought that one's temples could throb so? Give me a scent-bottle; I will bathe my temples with *eau de Cologne*, and try to be as calm and as happy as you can wish. Behold, we have acted our parts well, and now we will go and sit down in a corner; for people are already taking up their hats and umbrellas, and are moving on their seats. Good-night! Good-night!"

" Nicola, Nicola, collect yourself. This is bordering on madness, my poor darling!" cried Emma, throwing her arms around her friend and sobbing aloud; but Nicola continued—

" Do not fear for my reason, my child, for that I shall preserve only too well. But cry on, Emma. I would give a good deal of my

intellect if I also could cry, but I cannot and
must not. It is foolish to cry if one has not
the right thereto. Yes, to be sure, little
woman, you are well off, and God preserve
your happiness. You have always had everything intact and entire, laughter and tears,
and the two did not get into conflict with
each other. You were not called from all
sides, when you wanted to sit down on a stool
of your own; and they did not drag you
forward by the wings if you failed to heed
their shrill summons. You could always
quietly go on your way, and good people
have led and accompanied you. I do wish I
might have rocked my thoughts as well as
my babies like you; but as this was not to be,
love, you must set out to-morrow early and
give my compliments to my gracious lady
mother, and tell her that I have gone away
with that strange Mr. Hagebucher from
Tumurkieland, and that they please must not
mind it. Tell her further, that I could not

have borne to remain here, and that under
the circumstances, fresh air and change of
scenery would act very beneficially on my
character and mood. You may drop a hint
of the seven dwarfs behind the seven hills, or
some other well-known spot in fairyland,
whither neither letters nor telegrams can get.
You may add in a whisper, that, as all was
now lost, and there was no longer any hope
of further advantages and honours to be
attained, and as Princess Marianne under the
circumstances would surely not object to my
disappearance, mamma also would no doubt
make up her mind to it. If you like, you
may add that Nicola will certainly not go
and drown herself, so that if that's a comfort,
it is at their disposal; and that she would
write as soon as she felt able to do so, and
would moreover remain a dutiful and patient
daughter, if matters were not made too
difficult for her. You will know how to act
as my *ministre plénipotentiaire*, Emma Wild-

berg, and take my word—yes, all of you, take my honest, honest word—that I do not mean to make a romance out of my misery. Say that it were my intention to take to the digging of roots and the eating of acorns very seriously, in the wilderness, and that therefore there was nothing else for it than to let me go on my way. Then drop your curtsey and go home ; throw an old shoe after me for luck, and then sit down in a corner and think of a touching and instructive story for your children, and let it begin : ' Once upon a time there lived a young girl whose name was Nicola, and she had many a strange adventure with fairies, goblins, and wizards ; and she got lost in a wood, one hardly knows how, but it is very touching and instructive.' "

So spoke Nicola von Glimmern, pressing her clenched hands against her forehead, and only stopping from mere exhaustion and want of breath. Leonhard Hagebucher let

her talk on, never once trying to interrupt
her. Only when she dropped on the
cushioned divan, sobbing convulsively, he
said, as he put his head outside the window—

"It begins to snow. Bismillah, he who
wants to hide his footprints will find this
an excellent weather for travelling; and it
is my opinion also, *Frau Majorin*, that Mrs.
Nicola and I leave the town at daybreak, and
take our way over Nippenburg and Bumsdorf
to the cats'-mill. It is now very silent in the
woods around Fliegenhausen, as I have but
lately experienced. Nature has put her
finger on her lips, and nobody need fear the
jubilant voices in meadows and fields. We
will knock at Mrs. Claudine's door, and shall
be surprised to find how all other tones,
which but lately, sounded shrilly and harshly
in our ears, will die away. Mrs. von Wildberg does not know the cats'-mill, but Mrs.
Nicola knows it. There is no better place
on earth to carry a great sorrow to, and what

fire and iron cannot heal, our dear Lady
Patience, Mrs. Claudine, will heal with her
soft hand. There is not much to be said
about it. The chief thing is to know the
way, and I promise Mrs. Emma to be a
good guide to Mrs. Nicola, and to entertain
her on the way with my own grief which I
take with me to the cats'-mill."

Mrs. von Wildberg caught the African by
both his shoulders and gave him a hearty
kiss.

" You are an excellent man, Hagebucher!"
said she.

Nicola, rising from her reclining position,
held out her hand to her friend as she
said—

" You also! You spoke before, of some
grief you had met with. But I am both deaf
and blind. What have they again been
doing to you ? "

Leonhard almost felt some compunction
for having put his small misadventure beside

the misfortunes of this woman, though he
had done it with the best intention. Still
the remedy had taken effect, and drawn the
wife of the Baron von Glimmern out of the
deepest stupor.

"I will tell you and Mrs. Claudine the rest
in the mill, but now let us reflect how, and
in what way, we had best set out on our
journey."

It required much pains and a great deal of
persuasion, both kind and hard words, before
the excited Nicola could be convinced that
one could not start at that hour and under
such circumstances, but would have to wait
for the morning. It is not always that the
cool mind conquers the feverish one under
similar circumstances; grief and anger are
almost as obdurate opponents to reason, as
love, but this time, Hagebucher triumphed at
last. Like a tired child worn out with crying,
he left Nicola on her cushions, under the care
of her friend Emma, and then went to join

the two gentlemen, whom he found in exactly
the same position in which he had left them
half an hour before.

" How are the ladies? How is my poor
cousin ? " exclaimed the lieutenant. " Oh,
Hagebucher, I have waited more than once
with a beating heart before more than one
door ; but never in such a state bordering on
distraction as now. And, though I am a
good fellow, and easily to be persuaded that
a thing is either true or a fable, I cannot
with the best will believe in this Mr. van der
Mook ; and what regards the major, you had
best ask him yourself."

The major shook his head, and showed
himself once more a well-read man, as he
recited—

> " This
> Like a grape-shot gives me many wounds,
> And in superfluous manner brings grim death."

" I trust not," said Hagebucher, unable to
suppress a smile, in spite of all his cares, at

the eminently characteristic behaviour of the
two military gentlemen. "Victor Fehleysen
lives and has returned, and I trust this will
turn out to our joint satisfaction. You, friend
Bumsdorf, will first have an opportunity of
greeting the resuscitated one. We accept
your proffered help with both hands. You
must instantly set out for the cats'-mill, and
it will be your own look-out how you get
there safest and quickest. You must start
on the spot, to acquaint Mr. van der Mook
with all that has happened. He will understand what he has to do, and not await
Nicola's arrival under his mother's roof.
Above all, tell him of Glimmern's flight and
Lieutenant Kind's wild pursuit. The next
train in that direction only leaves to-morrow.
So you will have to make the way on horse-
back, if that can be done."

"I absconded with Prospero in similar
weather, and also at the dead of night," cried
the lieutenant, for the first time putting up

his eye-glass since the catastrophe, and looking with pleased eyes at the African. "The
crime succeeded perfectly, that is, the in-
dignant old man only fetched back the horse
from my stables here. Hagebucher, I thank
you most heartily. You have given me new
life with this commission. I shall ride as no
sane man ever rode before. I shall have to
put poor Roland to a severe test; and if he
and I do not break our necks, I shall be at
Nippenburg by six, and at the cats'-mill
between seven and eight."

"Then we are saved. In the afternoon I
shall arrive with Nicola at Mrs. Claudine's
door," said Leonhard.

The lieutenant had already put his sabre
into the right position, and now took up his
cap.

"Commend me to my cousin; in a quarter
of an hour I shall be in the saddle. I would
lame Pegasus himself, or the horse of the four
children of Haymon, for her sake. Poor
Roland!"

"Your papa, no doubt, will know how to appreciate the service likewise," said Hage-bucher, consolingly; and Mr. Hugo von Bumsdorf, allowing the glass to drop from his eye, exclaimed—

"*C'est vrai!*" and then added, "My dear friend, both as man and cavalier, I shall sacrifice the good animal without scruples, and shall likewise take pleasure in announcing your speedy arrival in your own house. *Au revoir* under pleasanter circumstances."

He strode off, and the major said—"Your message is in good hands, Hagebucher. I will take care to obtain the necessary leave for that madcap young fellow; but what else can I do? I feel so useless, and would like much to take an active part in this sad business."

Hagebucher shrugged his shoulders.

"What can any of us do? We spread out our cloaks on the way, but the path itself leads to Golgotha all the same. If the strength to bear the heavy burden were not

in the victim's own breast, all that we might
do towards softening the crisis would be useless; nay more, might do positive harm.
Go to the ladies now; there will be sufficient
opportunity for saying many a good and
earnest word. I will make my own preparations for the journey. If you could induce
the—patient to lie down for a few moments,
you would do a good deed."

As he had previously done to the lieutenant, the African also gave a short account
to Major Wildberg of Victor Fehleysen's
return; then stepped into Mrs. Emma's room,
where he found everything unchanged. He
certainly did not try to talk of reason,
heroism, and philosophy, but took a short,
hearty leave from Mrs. Emma, telling her
that he would be at the door with a carriage
at eight o'clock. Nicola von Glimmern
hardly seemed to notice his presence; and so
he left the house, and slowly wended his way
back to the Kesselstrasse.

CHAPTER IX.

THE town was now as dark and silent as only a small German Residence can be at that hour of night. The lamps at the street-corners and in the houses were all put out. With the exception of a few, the people who had received intelligence of the exciting event, had gone to bed; and these few sat in their corners, behind closed shutters, and certainly did nothing towards giving the town an aspect of liveliness.

The brightest, most wide-awake inhabitant of the town was perhaps at this moment the man from the Mountains of the Moon, Mr. Leonhard Hagebucher. He had inhaled a good breath of fresh air under Major Wildberg's gate, and tested the elasticity of his limbs by jumping across a heap of snow, and he had found them in first-rate condition. He felt relieved and free; something like a man who for a long time has carried a ball in his side, and who at length holds the uncomfortable bit of lead in his hand, leisurely contemplating it, and, if he likes, fastening it to his watch-chain, or making the deepest philosophical reflections on the relations of that piece of lead with his physical and moral man.

"I only wonder what Täubrich Pasha will say to this," said Leonhard Hagebucher as he reached his own door; and then another thought entered his head, which made him hurry upstairs all the quicker.

"By Jove, we have still other confessions to make each other. O *sedes sapientiæ*, how on earth did the fellow come to introduce Lieutenant Kind in this way at M. von Betzendorf's party?"

Hastily entering his room, he found the Jerusalemite lying with his arms on the congratulatory sheet and his nose on the bouquet, in utter absence of mind, and he himself started violently when the dreaming tailor uttered a loud cry of terror, as he tried to rouse him, by putting his hand on the latter's shoulder. The pasha uttered a loud yell, started to his feet, and bounded to the furthest corner, from whence he cast about terrified looks, and, with his meagre arms and hands described windmill-like evolutions in the air.

"Halloo! It is I! Come to your senses, Täubrich!" cried the African.

"Who? Who? Oh, Jesus, have mercy!"

Leonhard took the lamp from the table, stepped up with it to the tailor, and said—

"Please to convince yourself that nobody has the intention to devour you, and to carry you off through the chimney. Come to your senses, man—whom did you believe to see?"

"Always him—my—good friend—Lieutenant Kind," moaned the tailor. "Oh, God,
he always used to come in that way during
your absence—to—keep me—company. He
has worn me out with his—af—fection—and
this night he has completed his work, and
ruined my ner—vous system for all the days
to come."

"Come, Täubrich," said Hagebucher, per-
suasively, "let us sit down and speak of this
night. It was certainly rather exciting, and
you also have acted your part in it. How
did the lieutenant get into M. von Betzendorf's house?"

"As he always comes! He stood behind
me in the antechamber, and a dozen glasses
of lemonade went to the ground in consequence. I have said before, a rattlesnake is
an angel compared to him—oh, *he* doesn't
rattle! No thought of it! He is there, and
a man has no will of his own as long as he
keeps his eye on him. I stand amidst the

broken glasses, and he asks, just as he did the first time he was here to fetch you, Sidi, 'Is the gentleman at home?' and all else that I know, is that he takes hold of my arm, that I carry another tray in my hands, and that we push together through the ball-room, and that suddenly the entire festivity ends in terror and excitement, and all the gaiety becomes a terrible chaos."

"You stood with the lieutenant behind M. von Glimmern's chair?"

"I had to do it. He had led me there! It was as if he could not carry out his object without me. Yes, I stood behind the chair of his Excellency; and, when he jumped up and confronted the lieutenant, I dropped the tray for the second time; and then—then Mad. von Glimmern took my arm, and led me back through the ball-room, and that was still worse than crossing it with Lieutenant Kind."

The African gently tapped the man from Jerusalem on the shoulder, and said—

"I thank you; you have done very well, and have acted like a brave and faithful knight.",

"Did I really? Oh, Lord, I don't know whether I did; but I am very glad to hear it. My heart bled when the poor, beautiful lady clung to my arm; and I took the first shawl I could lay hands on in the cloak-room, and put it around her shoulders; but I do not think that she noticed it. How could I have thought that she would know me? But she did know me, Sidi, and pronounced my name and yours. Several of the ladies and gentlemen tried to stop her, or speak to her; but she only looked at them, and they started back terrified, and let us go on our way."

"And they did well," muttered Hagebucher.

"When we were in the street, she shuddered; and, speaking for the first time, she said, 'Where are we going, Täubrich?' I, of course, took the liberty to suggest home, or to her lady mother; but she shook her head, and replied that she had no longer any home, and did not wish to go to her mother. Oh, Sidi! I would have liked best to take her to the Kesselstrasse; but, then, that would not do, and so we went to Mrs. Wildberg— you see, I did not know any better—and thither she allowed herself to be led."

"The Lord always knows whom he is to entrust with a guardianship," said Leonhard, very seriously; and then added, with a smile, "Täubrich, many tailors will be born before another will see the light of this world fit to hold a candle to you. And now, allow me to offer you my best thanks for your congratulation, as well as this pretty bouquet."

Longer and longer the tailor stretched out his neck, and an indescribable grin lighted up his face; every muscle awoke like a winter-sleeper under the reviving rays of a spring sun.

"Oh, heavens! Oh, Jerusalem! I beg a

thousand pardons. *That* I had altogether forgotten!"

"Never mind, Täubrich," said Hagebucher.
"To tell the truth, I had intended to treat
you very savagely on account of your seductive
insinuations, your deceitful wiles; but, *video
meliora proboque*, that is, this time it won't
do, and we had better let the matter rest."

The pasha once more beheld a spectre,
and again retreated towards the wall.

"She won't have me, Täubrich," said
Hagebucher.

"She won't have you?" cried the tailor in
the highest treble.

"On no condition."

Täubrich Pasha sat down, passed both his
hands through his hair, and acted like a
professor of logic, who is able to explain all
that he wants to know in the heavens as well
as on earth.

"Reasons?"

"Ferdinand!" replied Hagebucher in a

hollow voice; and added, still more sub-
terraneously, "Zwichmüller;" upon which
Täubrich Pasha sank into an abyss, into
which we will by no means follow him, for
we should never have the strength or ability
to get out of it again and be our old self.

To be sure, it cost the African some pains
under these circumstances, to rouse him to
the necessary conscious activity; but when
he had succeeded in doing so, he became very
lively, in spite of his nervous dejection; gave
his advice clearly and distinctly, and received
his orders for the next hours with open eyes
and ears. By his help, Hagebucher stopped
before Major Wildberg's house at six o'clock
with a carriage. A new day broke over the
world, the paths of M. von Glimmern and
those of Lieutenant Kind, and, as a matter
of course, also over the path of Lieutenant
Hugo von Bumsdorf.

A thick mist lay at this time over and
between the hills of Fliegenhausen, and the

path was almost more difficult to find, and
more dangerous to follow, than in the first
hours after midnight, when the air was clear,
and the snow made the night a little less
dark. But Lieutenant Hugo von Bumsdorf
was an excellent rider, and what was of
almost greater importance under the present
circumstances, he knew his native scenery by
heart, having roved through hills and dales,
and played his pranks there, in the days of
his innocent childhood, as well as his less
innocent youth. He reached Nippenburg
half an hour sooner than he himself had
deemed possible, and cantered along, but
without being able to enjoy the thousand gay
memories which were connected with the
place and its drowsy Philistines. He scarcely
glanced up at the windows of the fair damsels
of the town; he did not even feel the desire
to play Uncle and Aunt Schnödler some trick;
but he felt very cold, and his duty did not
permit him to stop a moment before the

Golden Peacock, to rouse the whole house from their slumbers, in order to get a glass of Madeira. He likewise rode through Bumsdorf without stopping, and merely cast a longing look, first at the house of the late inspector of the customs, Hagebucher, and then across the garden walls at the sacred roofs on his father's estate.

"I would like to know who is kind enough to dream of me at this moment," muttered he. "Oh, Roland, my poor fellow, there they lie, warm and snug. Bah! it is immensely indifferent to me what the old man over there is snoring about; but as for little Lina—but forward, Roland! they will certainly open their eyes wide, when we have executed our commission, and shall present ourselves."

He once more applied the spurs to the tired animal, and sped on, muttering the names of Victor Fehleysen and Nicola, amidst curses on the Baron von Glimmern; and

whilst he was about it, cursing a good many
other things.

Thus he safely reached the cats'-mill a
little before seven, strangely moved by a
mixture of anger, sadness, and anxiety, and,
much to his relief, he beheld a light in the
cottage, shining out through the mist. So
somebody was already awake in the house,
and the messenger could make his report;
and, if he pleased, turn his horse's head, and
ride back to the Residence on the spot. But
he did not please to do so. Benumbed and
shivering, he painfully dismounted from his
perspiring horse, threw the remainder of his
cigar into the wood, and staggered through
the little garden towards the window from
which came the gleam of light. Much he
would have liked first to cast an inquisitive
look into the room ; but the ice-covered
panes prevented it, and so he had to knock
in order to obtain admittance. Instantly
somebody started up inside, upsetting a

chair, and a dark figure interposed itself between the window and the light.

"Friends!" exclaimed the shivering messenger, adding, "By Jove, 'tis plain that we were not expected."

By this time the door of the cats'-mill was opened, and Mr. van der Mook appeared on the threshold, revolver in hand, for which precaution his former life easily furnished an excuse.

"Pray do not put yourself out on my account," said the lieutenant. "My name is Bumsdorf, and I come from the Residence by order of my very good friend Mr. Leonhard Hagebucher, and if I have the honour to speak—with—Mr.—Mr. van der Mook—that is—Mr. Victor—— "

"I am Victor Fehleysen, or, if you prefer, the dealer in wild animals, Cornelius van der Mook," replied the other, with a surprised and distressful stare at the half-frozen young warrior. "What has occurred? As Hagebucher sends you, and as you know of my existence and name, please to step in, softly if you please, for my mother is still asleep, and, no matter what you bring, you must walk softly."

On entering the heated room, the lieutenant had almost sunk to the ground. Victor Fehleysen supported him, and placed him in his mother's arm-chair. The stove was red-hot, and a cloud of smoke from strong Turkish tobacco filled the room. On the table beside the lamp stood a coffee-machine, amidst a medley of geographical maps, books, and papers. Lieutenant Hugo von Bumsdorf had never before drunk so excellent a cup of coffee as that which Mr. van der Mook now offered him.

It took some time before the messenger was capable of delivering his message, but he had hardly pronounced the first words when a great change came over Mr. van der Mook, which would not have displeased the man from Tumurkieland. Victor Fehleysen had accosted the lieutenant with the same dogged sullenness with which he accosted all those whose hands he thought were against him, and the lieutenant had permitted himself, in the depth of his soul, to make the little flattering observation—"That seems to be a most repulsive sort of fellow; a pleasant companion to be shut up with in this den a whole winter. God help poor Nicola and Mrs. Claudine!"

As soon as he had recovered sufficiently, he first stated the most important part of his news, viz., that Mrs. Nicola von Glimmern was following at his heels, and then hurriedly continued his recital, as if he felt the want of getting away again as quickly as possible from his unsympathetic listener.

But the eyes of the said listener lighted up strangely; his breath came and went ever faster; he unbuttoned his waistcoat, and not that alone, but his heart also. Without interrupting the lieutenant, he listened intently, and only once murmured, " Oh, mother, mother ! "

Mr. Hugo von Bumsdorf certainly gave his account as objectively as anybody could have given him credit for. He entirely omitted his own views and feelings, as well as his favourite digressions into his own private life; and he even spoke of Lieutenant Kind, without thereby letting himself be decoyed into the territory of his own military experiences, sorrows, and joys.

Lieutenant Kind! Bah! Lieutenant Kind was already on his way, following at the heels of Baron von Glimmern, and Lieutenant von Bumsdorf's opinion was that the two gentlemen would be sure to meet somewhere. Lieutenant Victor von Fehleysen excitedly paced up and down the room, and looking irresolutely now at the revolver, which he had put on the table, then at the door, he softly said from time to time, " I am glad that I live! I am so glad that I live ! "

And now the door was opened, and Mrs.
Claudine entered hurriedly, looking pale and
excited. She first held out her hand to
Hugo, who had quickly risen, and then
locked her son in a close embrace.

The neighing and pawing of poor tired
Roland out in the snow had awakened her.
She had heard a strange man's voice below,
and fear and anxiety for her son had made
her leave her couch and hurry downstairs.
Outside the door, she already caught some
words and names which partially quieted her,
at the same time causing her deep emotion,
and now she stood there, looking from one to
the other, and cried—

"You must not withhold from me anything
that has happened. You rode all night,
Hugo, and Leonhard sends you. You spoke
of Nicola; what news do you bring my son
and me?"

"We do not intend to hide anything from
you, mother," said Victor, more gently than

was his wont. " You have conquered us all;
but you will once more have to make some
changes in your life. Nicola comes to you,
and I depart, but this time in peace, and I
know that you will not wish to detain me."

Mrs. Claudine was then told all that had
occurred in the Residence, and what was still
to come. Whilst the Lieutenant gave his
account, she sat there covering up her face
with both hands; but when Hugo for the
second time came to an end, she looked up
with eyes which, though glistening with tears,
were yet almost serene, and said—

" Yes, go, my son; I have long had to miss
you with great sorrow, but to-day I give you
my blessing ere you go, with a quiet heart.
You have but one path before you. Go and
try to prevent that that wretched man is not
treated worse by your old companion in
chains than justice demands. You cannot
live under the same roof with the wife of
Frederic von Glimmern. Go and be good,

my dear son. God has shown himself a just
God to us. Victor, Victor, do all you can
that no more blood be shed on our path; that
no other wild deed cry out to heaven for
vengeance. Think at all hours who, from
this time forward, will sit and walk by the
side of your old mother, and you will be a
brave as well as a strong and gentle man."

"Ay, you are right," sighed Mr. van der
Mook; "it is well as it is, I am bound to
admit it. I also thank my young comrade
here most heartily for his troublesome ride
this night. He drives me away from a warm
nest, you kind, old, proud mother; but I feel
as if I had slept a hundred years, and by all
that's living I am glad that I have awaked.
Life to me was like the wild dance of nightly
spectres, and I had forgotten the word which
would have banished them. Now another
has pronounced it for me from the distance;
and though I must once more go out into the
world, life is again mine, and I shall make

use of it, not like a wild, drunken, or insane man, but like a reasonable being and decent fellow."

For some moments Mrs. Claudine already had taken Lieutenant von Bumsdorf's hand, and now began to talk with him as if this hour were not rife with great and anxious matter for her. With motherly care she asked how he felt, and was very glad to hear that he had quite thawed by this time, and did not fear the least evil consequences from the fatigues of that night. She even had a word of sincere pity for poor Roland, and like Mr. van der Mook, Lieutenant von Bumsdorf became ever more convinced that Mrs. Claudine was indeed a great, proud soul.

At ten o'clock the lieutenant, riding the chestnut of the landlord from the Ox-tavern at Fliegenhausen, stopped before Hagebucher's house, and ere he turned his face homewards, he had a very pleasant though quite super-fluous chat with Miss Lina Hagebucher.

At eleven, Victor von Fehleysen had left the cats'-mill. Mrs. Claudine sat in her arm-chair, with closed eyes, listening to the footfalls that lost themselves in the distance, as well as to those which were approaching from thence. She prayed for all—for all; but who was praying for our dear Lady Patience?

CHAPTER X.

WE also stay to listen for a few moments to
the footfalls which go away and those that
approach; for we have now two paths before
us on which we can attain the goal of our
wanderings. We can follow Mr. Cornelius
van der Mook from hour to hour, from station
to station, and relate how he succeeded in
overtaking the Baron von Glimmern as well
as Lieutenant Kind, but how both nevertheless escaped him for ever; and how he, at
bottom, and according to the natural development of his character, was heartily glad of
the latter, though he dared not show this,
from a sense of shame. On the other hand,
we can take a second path, on which the

wild words, the harsh deeds, the evil complications will not meet ear and eye too gratingly and glaringly, and only show us from the veiled distance what this world is, in which we live and try to be happy, as well as exercise and develop all our powers and capacities. *In utrumque paratus*,—ready for both ways, we choose the latter, for we take it to be neither an art nor a pleasurable sensation to take notes at a criminal examination.

Leonhard Hagebucher arrived with Mad. von Glimmern in the woods of Fliegenhausen at the same spot from which the unconscious Mrs. Claudine had been carried to the cats'-mill. He led the closely-veiled Nicola through the woods, and no sound was heard around them, except that of the snow, that occasionally fell from some branch which had succeeded in freeing itself of its burden.

Let us see! In spring, summer, and autumn there was a continual splashing and rushing of the waters in the upper land. They were forced to fall in mad leaps over wheels; they were drawn upwards by artful machinery; and again dashed down from the heights, according to the will of man. They were forced from their natural beds into channels above and underground, and their clear, limpid floods were stained and dimmed. Like mankind, they had little enjoyment of their existence; it was a continuous torment, a joyless working by day and by night; and now we will hear what the solitary drops, which in the bewitched glen below were falling over the old broken mill-wheel covered with green moss, had to say of the life outside those mountains, of the din and bustle in the streets and market-places of Brabant, the court of the fair Richildis.

Hush! hush! The soft tinkling of the drops on the wheel had ceased in the snow-covered woods. It was long since Mrs. Claudine had counted the march of time by its rhythm; and who has the right to ask after the gay crowds in Brabant and the court of the fair Richildis?

Patience, Faith, and with them Victory, in its fairest shape, stood on the threshold of the cottage to receive the approaching sorrow-laden Nicola, and to say to her, "Be welcome, a thousand times more welcome than in the days when you came here with your brightest laugh. Be welcome; we two sisters will hold your weary head in our arms, and as long as you will not step beyond this threshold you need not fear the powers that drove you hither. Be welcome; we are called Patience and Faith. People talk much about us; but there are but few who know us, but he who is strong like her whom we watch over, will receive the crown from our sister Victory, which she has given to Mrs. Claudine."

In the cats'-mill one could hear no bell strike; but it was noon, and the peasant women at Fliegenhausen were putting the soup-dishes on the table, when the man from the Mountains of the Moon reached the mill with Mrs. Nicola.

Mrs. Claudine uttered no cry, and did not start up when the two entered. She only stretched out both her hands towards them, and exclaimed—

"My child, my dear, dear daughter! Now you have returned home, and now you are mine, and I shall never let you go from me again. Do you see that the lost—the dead—do yet return! They, who were chained with a hundred fetters in the most terrible captivity, may free themselves, or may be set free by their wicked masters with a scornful laugh. No, my daughter; now there is no one has any claim on your soul but myself. Do you hear? Not one! Not one! None near you and none in the distance. None in the past or in the future. No one in all the wide world. The ones

have given up all their rights on you, and
the others you yourself had to turn away
from. Now you must love me alone,—you
may only be my daughter, my child, for this
is the sweetest and best core of this great
sorrow, that if it were not so, you would not
have had the right to come to me. You are
still confused, but the hour is not far off
when you will believe in your own liberty.
Be quiet and have patience; the years pass
by like a day, that is an old saying; but we
are not always capable of realizing the whole
of its good and consolatory meaning."

In the beginning, Nicola heard nothing
but the sound of Mrs. Claudine's voice. She
could not understand the meaning of her
words ; but the hour was indeed not far off
in which the mother could speak in clearer
words of the return of her son, finding an
echo for the faintest thrill and emotion that
passed through her heart.

It was still a terrible hour for Nicola,

when the full understanding of her position
came to her. The disclosure took place at
twilight, when the mists and the shadows of
the wood were again shrouding the cats'-mill,
and Mrs. Claudine sat in her easy-chair, holding Nicola's head in her lap. The first
impression was overpowering, and the shock
almost greater than it had been during that
frightful scene in the ball-room at M. Betzendorf's. Slowly, with fixed, staring eyes,
Nicola von Glimmern rose and tore herself
away from the protecting arms of the faithful old woman, and, laughing wildly, she
cried—

"Mother, it was not right to hide this
from me! This also was a false game! Oh,
how cruel to bring me here, and then to tell
me that this spot, too, does no longer hold any
place for me. That there was no place left
for me in all the world, and that all was
finished, and everybody had had his share,
and I mine!"

Hastily tightening her shawl across her breast, she hurried towards the door, as if she could not stay another moment under the roof near the hearth of Mrs. Claudine, as if she must run out into the night at once, into the woods, into her grave, no matter whither and to what fate.

Once more she moaned aloud, half in pain and half in anger, but the latter was only directed against herself, and in this clear distinction between her feelings, lay her sole safeguard against madness, and this alone could deter her from another wild, aimless flight. Pain and grief, however, also belonged to Mrs. Claudine, and her power over the unhappy woman lay hidden in these. Softly, imploringly, and with tears in her voice, Mrs. Claudine called out her name, and then, she let go the handle of the door, and standing a few moments motionless, with both hands pressed against her temples, she rushed back and again lay on her knees before our

dear Lady Patience, once more hiding her
face in her lap, and letting her finish her tale
of how he came home, and all that he had
experienced, and how he had gone away joy-
fully and as a better man, and had relin-
quished the place near his mother with the
glad conviction that all would yet turn out
well.

The mother kept back nothing. She described her son just as he was, and did not
hesitate to paint him in every trait, as the
mad, wild life he had led had made him.
Not Leonhard Hagebucher, neither friend nor
enemy, could have given a more impartial
judgment. She stripped him of all glory
that did not belong to him; she did not withhold what he had ever lacked and what he
had lost since; but neither did she withhold
what he had learnt and acquired on his adventurous paths. She pointed out how Nicola
might help and influence him. She proved
how the presence of her who had become

homeless, near the heart and under the protection of his mother, was the greatest blessing, the best guarantee for the peace of him who had been homeless so long. Finally, she spoke of Lieutenant Kind, and Nicola nestled closer to her when this name was pronounced.

By this time, Nicola von Glimmern had also heard Lieutenant Kind's history. On her long, tearful way to the cats'-mill, Hagebucher had slowly and cautiously acquainted her with Lieutenant Kind's story, only omitting Mr. van der Mook's name. The precipices between which she had thus walked all unconsciously, suddenly revealed themselves to her, and with a shudder she gazed at the crowd of spectral arms which had risen around her, and that stretched out their ghastly hands for her from all sides.

A fear of spectres came over her, of which she never again could entirely free herself, and from that hour she never left a room or

closed a door behind her, without experiencing
a feeling in the depths of her soul as if, in
the empty place she had just left, a dread,
weird *something* rose up, and, looking after
her with a horrible demoniacal grin, hissed
out, "Do you think that you are ever alone
with yourself? We are here! We are here,
and look at you, and watch and mock you!
Not defiance and not shame will help you;
we see and hear you, and exult over you.
We are your enemies, and know that we shall
kill you yet with our looks!" The genii on
the threshold and near the hearth of Mrs.
Claudine had a difficult position to hold
against these enemies.

"I will remain, for I have no longer any
will of my own," said Nicola. "I have
driven him out once more, and usurped his
place. You say that it were well so, mother,
and I will try to believe it, but I cannot think
over it."

"It is well so," said Mrs. Claudine, and

she could say no more, for now there began
that state for Nicola which both conquerors
and vanquished must learn to know; that
stage during which all we can do for the
patient is to chase away the flies in summer,
and in winter to let him lie undisturbed, or at
the utmost to shake up his pillow.

It was no illness which had taken hold of
Nicola. It was only an indescribable weari-
ness and craving after sleep, during which
we are indifferent to aught but the creaking
of a door, the pushing away of a chair or
table, the noise in the streets, and the visits
even of our best friends. But of all these,
the weary woman in the wintry wood and
the bewitched mill was quite safe. The
cawing of the rooks and the cry of the wild
geese as they flew over the tree-tops, did not
disturb her; nay, it sounded like a comfort-
ing voice from nature's great, true realm, and
the wind also was like a soothing lullaby for
her.

Leonhard Hagebucher, the only one who, from the crowds of people who once had eddied around Nicola, was allowed to cross the threshold of the cats'-mill, did not disturb her. He came and went on tiptoe, and said but little. For hours he would sit in a corner or at the window, book in hand, but oftener gazing out into the woods than reading. And if any one had asked him of what he was thinking—of Aunt Schnödler, or the wise tailor, Felix Täubrich, of Mrs. Kulla Gulla at Abu Telfan in Tumurkieland, or Mr. Ferdinand Zwichmüller at Montreux on the lake of Geneva—the query would often enough have remained unanswered. Still there was one thing of which he had to think continually, and for which he waited at all hours with a sort of suppressed anxiety. This was a letter from Mr. Cornelius van der Mook, which this latter, to be sure, had never promised, but which was bound to come some

day—to-day or to-morrow, at breakfast or
supper-time, in the bright noon or at midnight, the hour when spirits are allowed to
walk the earth; which latter time might have
been the most suitable.

CHAPTER XI.

Is it not a strange thing that the cats'-mill
might be, and in fact is, anywhere in Germany, and that Nippenburg too is everywhere, and the one cannot well be imagined
without the other ?   Is it not a strange thing
that the man from Tumurkieland, the man
from the Mountains of the Moon, never makes
his appearance without Uncle and Aunt
Schnödler ?   Wherever we turn our eyes, we
always and everywhere find that German
genius derives one-third of its strength from
the ranks of the Philistines, and is crushed
by the old giant *Thought* it wrestles with
high up in the air, unless it succeeds in
touching the ground it sprang from, at the
right time.

There are the Sunday children of other
nations, whatever their names may be —
Shakespeare, Milton, Byron, Dante, Ariosto,
Tasso, Rabelais, Corneille, Molière—they do
not toil, neither do they spin, and yet
Solomon in all his glory is not arrayed like
one of these. But in the land from the
Vosges Mountains to the Vistula there is a
continuous work-day; the air is ever filled
with the scent of newly-ploughed fields; and
every spark of fire that rises heavenwards
has an earthly smell about it, which we trust
that the gods will be pleased to reward at
last! They all toil and spin, the great men
who march at the head of *us*, and they all
come from Nippenburg, no matter what name
they bear—Luther, Goethe, Jean Paul—and
they are not ashamed of their origin. On the
contrary, they like to show a kindly interest
and understanding for the workshop, the
office, and the counting-house, and even
Friedrich von Schiller, who of all our spiritual

heroes broke most entirely with Bumsdorf and Nippenburg, felt from time to time a hearty desire to be reminded by a homely "weisht"* of his familiar, native surroundings.

Long live Nippenburg and Bumsdorf! The beer-jug and the coffee-pot, the knitting and the inkstand! Hurrah for the ground we stand on, and in which we shall be buried! Hurrah for the knight of Bumsdorf, Uncle and Aunt Schnödler, Uncle Hagebucher, and Cousin Clementine; and above all, hurrah for Cousin Wassertreter!

The jovial Mr. Hugo von Bumsdorf had had no reason for making a secret of his mad ride to the cats'-mill, when he had returned to the comfortable Lares and Penates of his father's house. To be sure he had to account for his unexpected appearance, and he did so in the most thorough manner. He began

* The Suabian dialect for "weisst Du," do you know.

at the very beginning, and often digressed
into various side paths; but then he never
skipped anything of importance, or suppressed anything which might stir up the
abominable, stagnating, provincial waters.

And the province was stirred up! Nothing
like this had transpired since Leonhard
Hagebucher's return from African captivity,
and fully deserved to be put side by side
with this event, if it did not even surpass it
in general interest and importance.

From the Bumsdorf estate the news spread
over the Hagebuchers' house, and reached
Nippenburg on the wings of the wind, everywhere exciting an interest, such as is generally
only produced by the alarm-bell at a fire.
Cousin Wassertreter afterwards was fully
entitled to compare himself to Horatius Cocles,
who alone defended the Sublician bridge
against the army of King Porsenna. Like
that brave hero, he defended *solus* the high-
road to Fliegenhausen against the inquisitive

inhabitants of Nippenburg. Cousin Clementine, on the other hand, might have compared
herself, though in a different way, to the
celebrated virgin Cloelia.   It is true that she
did not swim across the Tiber ; but she cir-
cumvented Cousin Wassertreter in company
of ten other elderly maidens, and actually got
as far as the Ox-Tavern at Fliegenhausen,
where she unfortunately was intercepted by
Leonhard Hagebucher, and sent back with
the notice ; that the Baroness von Glimmern
was as yet unable to receive any visitors.

During this time Cousin Wassertreter was
again the sole comfort and support which
Leonhard found outside the cats'-mill, being
also the only one with whom the African
could speak of the events of this latter time
without being interrupted by a flood of inter-
jections, and finally floored by a similar flood
of questions.   Cousin Wassertreter, as a
man who had seen old Goethe from behind,
simply said—

"My boy, you have acted your part very
well, and, moreover, it is my opinion that
you will now be a fixture here, just as I
became, after they set me free with the aforesaid official kick. Never mind, *he* also had
to sit in Weimar, and the world had to come
to him. Oh, dear me! Nippenburg has its
unspeakable merits, and you may still become
town-clerk; and if that will not satisfy your
ambition, we might obtain the title of town-
secretary for you. Then you will take to cul-
tivating pinks or dahlias, and, after having
suitably married your sister, you will by
degrees become great and venerable amongst
your nephews and nieces, as well as in the
Golden Peacock, where your father's chair
awaits you with open arms. I believe Lucifer
himself would not hesitate one single moment,
after the experiences he has made, if they
were to wink at the matter and offer him a
similar situation in the heavenly regions
above."

What the man from the Mountains of the
Moon replied to the malicious, grey-headed
old boy, history has not recorded; but it is
certain that he knew how to find out the
simple, but deeply philosophical thought that
lay at the bottom of his observations, and
carried them away with him to Bumsdorf,
there to reflect upon their meaning. He
really needed some consoling promises of a
pleasanter and calmer future very much, for,
in spite of the quiet which now reigned in
the house of the late inspector, it was a very
restless abode at present.

The old lady, his mother, grieved sorely
over the loss of the subtracting and adding
old grumbler; and if the forty years she had
lived with him had been a somewhat heavy
burden, she missed him dreadfully for all that,
and looked for him in every corner where
she formerly would not at all have liked to
find him. There is something mournful
about " the sound of a voice that is still," even

though the voice had something harsh and
grating about it. One may listen for footfalls
which one was wont to hear with real longing,
and the certainty that we shall never again
hear them, in the passage or the adjoining room,
may have something very mournful for us.

The " father " was missed by the old woman
wherever she was, and her son could not
make up to her for him who was gone. Yes,
Aunt Schnödler, Cousin Clementine, and Uncle
Sackermann were a much greater comfort and
more agreeable company for her than the
silent, absent-minded Leonhard. With the
former we could at least sit down and talk of
that which had been. Ah! the world was
entirely changed, and death had put everything out of its accustomed place. The old
lady had had to obey and give way continually
as long as her old man had led his cross
existence; but for all that she went about rest-
lessly, ever repeating that there was no better
or dearer place for her, than that beside his

grave, and that she would like nothing better than to rest there beside him now that he had gone away, who alone had ever thought of her welfare.

Treading softly, the African followed his mother about from place to place, and it cost him no little pains to put up with the thousand tearful or fretful whims and caprices. On many a dark and stormy day he sent his pale, depressed little sister away to her friends at the Manor; and Mr. Hugo von Bumsdorf, who had succeeded in getting his leave of absence prolonged, was very grateful to him for this.

They were very different fancies which the man from Tumurkieland indulged in, sitting near the window of the cats'-mill, to those which he brooded over when at home. Now and then he received long epistles from the Residence. Täubrich Pasha's letters were longing and incomprehensible; those of the professor grim and melancholy, and sometimes also rather unintelligible; but one thing was evident from the confessions of both his correspondents : the excitement about the events of these last weeks was still great in the Residence, and as to the private excitement of the two excellent individuals, this had by no means abated.

Leonhard answered as well as he could. He tried to cheer up the pasha with the prospect of a speedy and joyful meeting, meanwhile appointing him heir to his chief belongings in the Residence. The professor, who had announced to him the agreeable presence (hicuïtas he called it) of the amiable Mr. Ferdinand Zwickmüller, he comforted by alluding to his speedy departure, and further held out as a bait, that Bumsdorf, like so many another place, owed its origin to the Romans; inviting him to come over during the holidays, after his daughter's wedding, in order to convince himself personally of the accuracy of this statement, and to fetch the stone which proved it a fact.

What was the meaning of all this? There
have been people who, on the sands or on a
rock near the shore, were overtaken by the
flood, saw the waves rise, and still were
capable of keeping their pipe lighted, and
winding up their watch ere the merciless
waters rose up to their waistcoat-pocket.
They were by no means the weakest characters
who could do that; and the chances to be yet
saved from the impending danger, were
perhaps greater for them than for all those
who at such times have nothing but a despairing wringing of hands, and a dull stare
upon the grey, deadly water-desert. Mr.
van der Mook would be sure to write one
of these days, and the simplest and most
natural thing was to wait for the postman's knock as quietly as possible, and not
go further to meet him than was absolutely
necessary. In the beginning of February,
Mr. van der Mook's letter did come, and
ran as follows :—

"Southampton, on board the *Borussia*.

" MY DEAR HAGEBUCHER,

"As you know, I happen to possess rather a tough nature, and so I feel as well as circumstances will permit; but then, circumstances are bad enough, and, devil take me, if I know what faces you and others—whom I do not dare to name—will make, when you read this letter. When we two met at Abu Telfan in the kingdom of Darfur, and I had the pleasure of offering you my scant assistance in a not over pleasant situation, we could have no idea what agreeable burdens fate was yet going to put upon our joint shoulders. I am just now trying to strangle the beast which dwells within me with both hands, but for all that it would be well nigh miraculous if it did not show itself in that which I have to tell, and so you will have the pleasure of going to the mill, to bring to the mournful souls, the two poor women, the dirty, bloody rag wrapt up in clean linen.

" In Paris I did not find what I sought for, and of this I was rather glad, for I have spent a jolly time there in former days, and in this miserable world one does well to keep such green, innocent spots of memory undefiled. *Bon*, I have hunted both men and animals in my time, and do not lose the track so easily, if I care for the life, the skin, or the feathers of the game. In the streets I met an old acquaintance of mine, an Englishman, who, like myself, has become a staid man with time, and allows himself to be honestly supported by his wife. The lady has founded a very useful and lucrative establishment, address : Lying-in Villa, Rue Chateaubriand, No. 14 (no sign), and *Monsieur* takes his walks on the *Boulevards*, and has some time to spare for an old friend. We are both quite up to the game, but for all that, arrived too late at Havre to cross the Channel in the same boat with Lieutenant Kind. Miss Julia Brown has just arrived from Lancashire on matters

which will brook no delay, and has been
earnestly recommended to my companion's
wife in the *Rue Chateaubriand*. So Mr.
Smith had of course no longer any time to
spare for me; he had to accompany Miss Julia
home, and did so. I enjoy a very stormy
passage, land safely at Dover, and soon afterwards have the pleasure of seeing and hearing
below my windows in Piccadilly the current
rush on, in which I am to catch the two
drops you wot of.

"That I set about my task with some re-
pugnance, you will understand, *mon cher*, and
that my fate was sure to press me down into
the mire as deep as possible, became clear to
me as soon as I had turned my back on the
cats'-mill and your confident-looking face.
My dear friend, I dare say you guess what I
have to tell you. It was a short chase; and
my comrade has been so eager and quick that
I could not even be present at the end. So
once more, with the very best intentions, I

remained a neck's length behind, and, by my
soul, I grieve less that I cannot return to you
and boast of my achievements, than that such
a strong and honest life was wasted upon such
base, despicable game. My comrade, oh, my
comrade! my dear, brave companion in suffer-
ing and chains! Bah, I verily believe he is
better off than I!

" The London policemen are very pleasant
people. Years ago I had the pleasure of
making their acquaintance in another matter;
but that was something which did not much
regard me then, and is certainly of no importance now. After having searched several
days, like a sewer-hunter, and not been successful, nothing was left for me, as time
pressed and my restlessness increased from
hour to hour, but to leave my card in Bow
Street at the police-office, and to ask for the
advice and assistance of the gentlemen there.
This I did, and found them most obliging and
willing. I was introduced to a quiet, taciturn

gentleman, Inspector Cuddler, who was
placed at my disposal, and whom I shall no
doubt still often fancy to have by my side on
lonely walks. He quietly puts on his gloves,
takes his umbrella under his arm, and we
step out into the streets like two good friends
and worthy cockneys, who have made up their
minds to pay a visit to the lions at the Tower.
We wander on and on ; from day into night,
and again into another day. On foot, in
omnibuses, in cabs ; we find traces which are
lost again, reappear and vanish in a circle—
in zigzags. We take leave of each other
with a shake of the hand, and meet the
following morning at a place agreed upon.
From Belgravia to St. Giles's, from Pimlico
to Islington ! We hold conferences and take
notes at the police-stations of Westminster,
Marylebone, Southwark, and Thames Street.
Nothing ! nothing ! The matter would have
become tiresome for an *amateur ;* but I, who
was no *amateur* this time, held on, and Mr.

Cuddler, who seemed to have nothing else on earth to do, likewise. We waited at street corners, in coffee-rooms, and at last met with an apparition in the Haymarket amongst the Babylonian women. A gentleman gets into a cab there, and I give my Inspector a nudge. We have not the right to arrest Mr. Frederic von Glimmern, for nobody has denounced him; but 'a kingdom for his address!' We throw ourselves into another vehicle, and instruct the coachman; but Erin is of course three-quarters overboard, *i. e.*, completely drunk, and so we are upset against an orange-stall, and I go home to my tea, once more disappointed.

"But why need I detain you any longer? The scene is in Lower Thames Street, in the third storey of a third-rate hotel; time, midnight; weather, rainy and stormy. The house is in fearful excitement. Murder! Screams! Darkness! and the police have forced open the door of No. 26. At eleven

o'clock, Mr. Thomas Giblets, the inhabitant
of No. 25, heard the gentleman, his next-
door neighbour, come home, but not alone,
—and Mr. Giblets' attention was kept alive
for some time by a violent altercation, to
which he listened with a certain enjoyment
from behind his *Economist*. He, Mr. Giblets,
had had a hard day's work, and it added to
his momentary comfort to find that other
people also had their unpleasantnesses, and he
found, as he afterwards declared, the matter
only somewhat extraordinary, when, about
simultaneously, two pistol-shots were fired off,
followed by the fall of two heavy bodies and
other ominous sounds.

" The whole house was alarmed, and at
about two o'clock, Inspector Cuddler rang the
bell at my house in Piccadilly. I leave it to
your own imagination, *carissimo*, to fancy what
I found in Lower Thames Street. We, who
have both witnessed more than one fight and
battle, and have both now and then stood

between pools of blood without asking much
after the morality of the thing, yet retain a
certain ticklish sense for the picturesque, and
Mr. von Glimmern's room was that, when I
entered it.

" They had both returned and discussed
their affairs quite peaceably, after Lieutenant
Kind had locked the door and thrown the
key out of the window. So peaceful had they
been, that their exchange of words only added
to the comfort of their next-door neighbour.
And then they had agreed to exchange bullets
across the table, thus settling all differences.
They were found on either side of the table,
pistol in hand. It was discovered that my
friend, His Excellency Baron Frederic von
Glimmern, was shot through the heart, like
Alp the renegate of Venice, and that my
friend and comrade, the retired officer of the
Strafcompagnie at Wallenburg, Friedrich
Kind, was not hit so well, but likewise re-
moved from all earthly pains and troubles.

He lived half-an-hour after the door was forced open, and showed himself very tractable, gentle, and resigned. He died on Mr. von Glimmern's bed, for fifty years the only real soldier of the German confederate army. When I arrived with my companion, I found a city missionary by the corpse. The man, through his profession, has more opportunity for seeing strange sights, than most other people, and he who kneels down beside the rotten straw of Bethnal Green and Spitalfields, may have a word to say on the mysteries of death. In the first quiet moment that offered, I gave him a short explanation of the case before us, and he called it—tragically refreshing! When some years will have passed by, I shall decide whether I find it more tragical or more refreshing. At the present moment I suffer still too much from the influences of the odour of blood on my organs of taste and smell, and shall, therefore, as yet keep back my vote.

" Some further formalities the German and

English authorities will see to, and I have not much to add in this respect, except that the two corpses had decent burial, and that I succeeded in preventing their being put into the ground side by side, by which I believe I have acted according to the wishes and inclinations of both parties.

"And now let us become as sentimental and soft-hearted as the occasion requires! The grey waves are dashing against the sides of my ship, and my thoughts accompany this letter over the vexed sea to the German coast. I imagine the most different circumstances under which this letter may reach you, and what you will say after its receipt. I believe I have got the fever, or something like it. By Allah! an opium-trance, a battalion arrayed for battle, an Arab steed, and the prospect of the seventh heaven of the Prophet, these are the four things out of which, since the creation of the world, the only sensible and pleasant moments of mankind have been derived! By

Allah, I wish I were buried on some old or new Turkish battle-field, and were at rest !

"What will they say in the mill? What will they do ? Oh, Hagebucher, I have still the most intense longing to tear up this frantic epistle, and to come myself, and myself to look in at the window and listen at the door! Away with that thought! I believe I would come if I had played a part in the bloody tragedy in Lower Thames Street, and could say, 'This I did !'

"I whip this thought about in a circle, as a boy does his top! My poor girl, what will *she* say, when you will enter her door and say, 'He is dead?'

"By all the powers of darkness I do not know what is to be done, and that you, Hagebucher, you the stranger, should be able to pronounce that clearly and distinctly in the sleepy hollow, what is torturing my heart and maddening my brain! Maybe that it is

so.   Farewell, and give my love to my
mother.

"VICTOR FEHLEYSEN.

"P.S. I have become a woman, and have,
therefore, attained the right of adding a
postscriptum.   At one o'clock past noon, the
Borussia, which did not stop at Southampton
on my account, will set out for New York.
I am on my way to General Grant.   They
say that that gentleman possesses many a
good remedy against weak nerves and con-
gestions of the brain, and that he gives them
away cheap.

"CORNELIUS VAN DER MOOK."

One day and one night Leonhard Hagebucher pondered over the contents of this
letter.   Deep sank one scale of the balance,
whilst the other went high up, and he found
the lighter weight a heavy, heavy burden,
when he went to the two women in the cats'-
mill the next day.

CHAPTER XII.

"This is awful, and not at all what I expected," groaned the professor and doctor of
philosophy, George Christian Reihenschlager,
wiping off the perspiration that was stream-
ing down his forehead with his handkerchief,
and then looking along the high road, with
his spectacles pushed up. "The way seems
to get ever longer the further we go. I
never could stand dust; the sun is unbearable
in spite of my umbrella, and I had better not
mention the state of my feet. Täubrich, if
it were not one of my principles to carry out
everything I have once begun, if possible, I
would declare myself perfectly unable to
reach Nippenburg entirely on foot, laughing

to scorn all the teachings of the Stoic school. Do you understand me ? "

" I believe so; but I am not quite sure," said Täubrich Pasha, staring at the learned man with his customary melancholy shake of the head.

" You believe to understand me, but are not quite sure. Well, desire is either instinctive or reasonable. From this, according to the properties of the subject, there spring four passions or moods, and a threefold volition, with regard to which you may read the necessary details in Cicero's Tusculan conversations. A wise man directs his desires according to the latter, and in this consists the apathy of the Stoics, and therefore we will most certainly reach Nippenburg on foot. Do you now understand me ? "

" Perfectly ! " cried the tailor and factotum, with a merry bound into the air, and then added that, as for the heat, that was nothing. In Palestine one could learn that, and every path came to an end, and Nippenburg might easily be reached before dinner-time, if one did not stop at every stone, or stumble over it. With a deep sigh the Professor gathered up all his physical and mental strength, and followed the fleet-footed tailor on Cousin Wassertreter's dusty high-road in the direction of Nippenburg, Bumsdorf, and Fliegenhausen. And now, ere we describe their entrance into Leonhard's native place, we will state how the droll pair came to be together on the high road.

The professor had lived through a good many experiences since last winter. His friend Leonhard had for the second time deserted him and the Coptic grammar in the most shameless way, and his daughter, as may be imagined, had led her Ferdinand to the altar at Whitsuntide, and was superintending her household with great energy in the international school on the *Lacus Leimanus*. The whole world had turned

topsy-turvey, and the professor often did not
know where his head was, and there was
nobody left to set him right, except the
pasha, who, to be sure, was a man and coun-
sellor one could rely upon on all occasions.

It is true that his daughter, as well as his
son-in-law, had proposed to him to accompany them to Switzerland, and help to raise
the international college to the acme of
learned perfection; but at this he had become
almost rude, and called upon all the gods of
Latium and Hellas that nothing on earth
would ever induce him thus to sin against
true German thoroughness. Therefore he
gave his daughter as much of his fatherly
blessing as he had to dispose of, and let her
go, without accompanying her any further
than the door; afterwards locking himself up
in his study, and, for the time, entirely dis-
appearing from the world of the living.
Mould gathered on his ink, and worm-dust
under his chair; dust on his papers, and an

ever increasing cloud of ill-humour on his
brow. The work at the important book,
which at no time went on with the speed of
steam, by degrees came to a dead stop. The
house became as silent as the interior of a
pyramid, the old professor himself represent-
ing the mummy in the deepest, darkest
sepulchre, and Täubrich thoughtfully stood
on the threshold like some melancholy ibis,
dreaming of Nile plants and crocodile eggs,
and having but one answer for all persons
demanding admittance—

" The professor does not receive any
visitors."

It will ever remain an undecided question
which of the two musty Egyptians first con-
ceived and expressed the great thought of
paying a visit to their friend from Tumurkieland, in his native place, that is, Bumsdorf.
The thought was certainly a happy one, and
the Roman stone at Fliegenhausen had, no
doubt, its share in the fact that it was not

put aside, but ever gained more distinct out-
lines. A few tempting letters from Leonhard
also increased the longing after the man from
the Mountains of the Moon. In the beginning of June the wish to pay him a visit had
become a determination, and in the beginning
of the dog-days, all the necessary preparations
for the exciting and adventurous expedition
had been made. Nothing whatever stood in
the way of the plan, and so they really did
start one fine morning.

For twenty years the professor had not
got beyond the nearest surroundings of the
Residence, the well-known promenade and the
bronze grand-duke, and he had no idea what
he was doing, when, with antique daring, he
decided in favour of a "walking tour."
Everybody has heard of the grains of wheat
found in the hand of some mummy, which,
after having rested there for three thousand
years, were put into the ground and began
to sprout gaily, developing ears which bore

a rich crop of grains. A similar awakening now came to the feelings and sensations of that old Copt.

He had buried his wife, and now he had also got rid of his daughter. He fetched his *Ziegenhayner* * out of the corner in which it had rested for more than forty years, hunted up his old *Commers-book*, and hummed *Frei ist der Bursch! Frei ist der Bursch!* He then placed the *Ziegenhayner* on the table beside the *Commers-book*, and with folded arms stood looking at both as the noble knight of la Mancha may have looked at his sword and buckler on the evening before he first set out on his adventures. The pasha packed up the same knapsack which had accompanied him through the Syrian desert, and filled a flask, which had likewise seen a good deal of service, with some refreshing liquor. In the sacred grey dawn the two

* A walking-stick made of cherry-wood, and coming from Ziegenhain, near Jena, in Saxony.

heroes crept out of the house on tiptoe, leaving it with all its learned, and other dust and cobwebs to the care of the maid-servant, and slunk along the walls until they reached the town-gate like two escaping criminals or bolting school-boys; emerged into liberty and fresh air, and walked on — we know whither.

We likewise know that the road to Nip-penburg is not very long; that all the paths of this state cannot be long, both from geographical as well as political reasons; but for all that our two wanderers saw wonders on them. A snail, who has some important business to transact in the top of a poplar, hardly encounters more obstacles, difficulties, and reasons for stopping on its way, than our Coptic scholar on his. We cannot but regret that we are no longer in the beginning, or even the middle of our book, in order to do full justice to this walking expedition. They stopped two. nights on their way, and the

third morning found them in the aforesaid
mood, approaching Nippenburg, and we will
hasten on before them, in order to witness
their entrance into that celebrated place from
Cousin Wassertreter's windows.

To begin with, everything at Nippenburg
was still as it had been when we began our
veracious and wonderful story. The arms of
the town were still a grey and white stock-
ing in a blue square, and Uncle and Aunt
Schnödler still acted as shield-bearers, and
filled this post quite as well as the two well-
known wild men, the lion and unicorn, or
the two golden griffins of the House of Haps-
burg. As to Cousin Wassertreter, he was
still an abomination and thorn in the flesh
to the whole community.

As usual, Cousin Wassertreter stood leaning out of his window, and from a very
long pipe whiffed airy little cloudlets into
the eleventh hour of the morning, dividing
his attention between the very bad pave-

ment—which, by the way, did not the least
regard him—and Cousin Clementine Mauser,
who was just courting her canary; and in
order to have some little fun, he longingly
waited for the return of the boys from school.
Only he who has ever seen a salmon troubled
with worms, jump up from the depths of the
river, can form an adequate conception of
the way in which Cousin Wassertreter started
up, when, five minutes after eleven, in the
midst of the schoolboys boisterously escaping
from Rector Hauenstein, Professor Reihenschlager and his companion became visible on
the horizon—that is, the nearest street corner.

"Oh, heavens!" sighed Cousin Clementine.

"Thunder and lightning!" cried Cousin
Wassertreter, one moment later, first losing
one of his slippers on the stairs, and then
his pipe outside the door, and, like another
erl-king, "with crown and tail," that is, in
his night-cap and long ragged dressing-
gown, rushed out into the street, to embrace

his old chum, with an enthusiasm which threatened to choke him.

"Mushroom! Mushroom! Is it possible?"

"Oh, Skimmer, I believe so, but I hardly know!"

"What a pair of ruffians!" moaned Cousin Clementine.

But the road inspector did not take the trouble to introduce them to her from the street, but, seizing one with each hand, he dragged them through the circle of surprised Nippenburgers who had already assembled around the new-comers, into the house and upstairs; placed one into an easy-chair and the other on the sofa, roused the whole house for refreshments, and ever repeated—

"I do not yet believe it! I cannot believe it as yet!" And then he sent to the Golden Peacock, and ordered a dinner as splendid as they could manage to provide at so short a notice, threatening the Peacock with his curse in case of disappointment.

The professor found Nippenburg, as well
as the Skimmer, just as he had expected to
find them.   By half-past twelve he had
drank a little more wine than was good for
him, and when it was three he felt somewhat unsteady on his legs.   From four till
six he had a delightful nap on Cousin
Wassertreter's sofa, whilst the latter put a
thousand questions to the pasha with regard to the journey, rubbing his hands
ever more gleefully as this examination pro-
ceeded.

" He is the most capital old boy that ever
set his heart on the Coptic, and as soon as
he awakes we will march to Bumsdorf," cried
the inspector.   " Hurrah! this is still better
than old Goethe from behind.   And he shall
have his Roman mile-stone ; for though I
very much suspect that to be one of my own,
it is all the same for the matter of that, and
I am quite ready to swear to twenty more.
Hurrah!   Vivat!"

"Raise the *Schläger* * brightly gleaming,
Pierce the hat, and thus redeeming
Here the pledge in golden wine."

And, still half asleep, the professor responded from the sofa—

"Thus I pierce the hat, and swearing
Like an honest *Bursch*, declaring
Truth and honour ever mine."

The poplars on the road to Bumsdorf were casting long shadows when the two hoary college-friends were trudging along, to look up the man from the Mountains of the Moon, in a similar mood and a gait as unsteady as that in which they had often set out in the old days for the *Rasenmühle* or *Stiftsmühle*.†
The pasha also walked rather crookedly, and more than once stretched out his hand for an imaginary wall, in order to keep his

---

* A sort of rapier with which the German students fight their duels.

† Two favourite resorts of the students. The former, at Jena, has lately fallen a victim to the first railway built there; the other still exists in the neighbourhood of Heidelberg.

balance; whilst all three carried their hats in their hands, and were fanning themselves with them. They were able to hear the grass grow; they knew of more things than other people dreamt of in their philosophy; but they never thought that by their jovial existence they guaranteed a future *Gemü-hlichheit* for many thousand years to the German nation, just as three acorns, which a man holds in his hand, may represent an entire forest.

And now the low steeple of Bumsdorf peeped forth above the tree-tops, just as the red sun-ball glided down the horizon. Yet a few steps, and they, the professor, the cousin, and the pasha, gazed from the very same place into the elder-bower, where Leonhard after his return had looked in, to the great fright of his sister, the fair Nicola, and the two girls from the Manor. With a little cry of terror, Miss Lina Hagebucher started up also this time, and——

"Thunder and lightning!" cried Lieutenant Hugo von Bumsdorf, who, in a grey jacket and high top-boots, sat opposite the maiden, entertaining her in the most fluent manner of his progress in farming, Herr von Liebig, and his own future rational draining.

"Bismillah! God is indeed great, and Mahomed verily is his Prophet!" exclaimed Leonhard Hagebucher, making his appearance a few minutes later, with a long pipe in his hand, and bearing a strong resemblance, in feature as well as carriage, to his late father. But, very different from the old man, he crossed the intervening space from the house to the garden gate, in order to give the most cordial reception to his friends. The cat on the window-sill in the first floor, stopped trimming itself, and looked with unmistakable interest at Täubrich Pasha and the blue tasseled fez of the latter. The old lady in her mourning weeds took off her spectacles in evident surprise, putting them between

the open leaves of Schmolke's " Morning and
Evening Devotions," and, full of curiosity,
stepped forth to take her share of all the
greetings and introductions. She at once
took a great fancy to the professor, with his
old-fashioned compliments, his serious ways,
and fine, learned speeches, which often were
quite unintelligible to her. With regard to
the dreamy tailor, she could never, during
the whole time of his stay, quite get over
a certain fear of him; and always looked at
him timidly askance; and, shaking her head,
she confidentially stated that she did not
quite trust that man, who was either cleverer
than the professor, or much sillier than the
lame Hans from the Manor, Baron von
Bumsdorf's favourite; and that, if he were
neither of these, he must certainly be a great
scoundrel and first-rate actor, or a very
honest fellow, who only lacked a little of
that, of which most people had not got too
much, significantly tapping her forehead.

Who else looks over the hedge of the Hagebuchers' garden, and exclaims—

"Well, that is a surprise such as I like!" Who else could it be than the terrible dynast of the place, the grim, merciless practitioner of old feudal rights, the bloodthirsty knight of Bumsdorf? And what does he do to increase the terror which his appearance has called forth? He adds the cold mockery of speech to the horror of his presence, and turning to the youngest of his daughters, following close at his heels, he exclaims—

"Quick, Minny! Sievers has just left the Manor. Now prove that you know how to run. Quick! the carps are under no circumstances to go to the town. Sievers shall bring back the basket, and the Golden Peacock may look out how it can do without fish to-day. Forward—march! And stop—tell your mother that if she wants to see something very curious, she must come over at once to the African, where half of Egypt and the whole of Turkey have just arrived, and are to be seen gratis! . . . Good-evening, professor! Good-evening, Täubrich Pasha! We have talked of this honour and pleasure ever so long, but we have hardly believed in it."

Any one whose hand was shaken by the knight of Bumsdorf, retained the sensation for some time, and any one who was run and called after by Miss Minny, on the Nippenburg high road, had to be very swift of foot and hard of hearing to escape her. Sievers, the vassal, certainly did not escape her, and the Bumsdorf carps, to the great vexation of the landlady of the Golden Peacock, did not get to the kitchen there, but returned to the Manor, where they were eaten by the natives, as well as the two notables from the Residence, their dear and honoured guests. Only on the third day after his arrival in the province, Professor Reihenschlager thought of the Roman stone at Fliegenhausen, and, striking his forehead, he exclaimed—

"I declare, if I didn't feel all the time as if I had come here for a special purpose! By the Bucolics of Virgil, this comfortable life and fine fresh air do not at all seem to agree with me. In the building up of my different hypotheses on the nasal sounds in the European languages, and to which aborigines we owe them, I have not made the least progress, which strikes me as rather dangerous. I earnestly beg and entreat you, friend Hagebucher, to let me have my Roman mile-stone. It would really give me immense pleasure to prove the existence of the *urbs* at Bumsdorf, and under these circumstances I would not regard the time I have spent on this short but adventurous expedition, as entirely lost."

"Bravo, Mushroom!" laughed Cousin Wassertreter.

Leonhard Hagebucher laughed also, but not quite so boisterously, whilst the pasha sorrowfully let his underlip hang down, and Mr. Hugo cried—

" We have a wheat-field in the *Fuchsrücken*, and can make a picnic of the expedition. We'll pack the necessary sandwiches, the girls, wine-bottles, and ourselves on a waggon, and make coffee under the ' Gallow's Oak,' or near ' the Dead Man,' or some other romantic spot. The professor gets his stone, and we all pledge ourselves most solemnly to adopt his views and opinions on the matter. Afterwards we'll play blind man's buff, that is, whoever likes may join ; even the girls are not excluded from the game."

" Hear ! hear ! " cried Cousin Wasser-treter.

" If that isn't a most impudent fellow," said Miss Sophie von Bumsdorf, quite seri-ously.

" And in the evening we'll drive home," continued the Lieutenant; and then added aside, " By moonlight of course, Miss Lina ;

and if I am very much entreated, I'll take my bugle with me. Whoever has anything to object to in this project, will please state his reasons at once, so that we may prove to him the utter absurdity of his objections."

"*Accedo ad talem!* I vote unconditionally with the young man," said the professor, rising from his chair with all the dignity of a cardinal who has to elect a pope in solemn conclave; and all who were present enthusiastically followed his example. As it had been planned it was carried out, after every one had eagerly proposed some amendment to the plan.

The pasha sat with folded hands on a felled tree, vacantly staring at an oak opposite. Hagebucher had stretched out his long legs beside him. Further below, the professor, Cousin Wassertreter, and Sievers, the vassal, worked tremendously to clean the stone—which Cousin Wassertreter trusted less than ever—from the accumulated dirt of centuries; whilst higher up, on a green meadow, beside a bright fire and the coffee-pots, the girls were laughing with Mr. Hugo, and the dynast was inspecting his corn-fields with evident satisfaction. In the beginning, a soft rustling had been audible in the tree-tops, but now all was hushed.

"Well, Täubrich, what does the jackdaw up in the tree yonder say to you?" asked Leonhard, quickly rising before he had finished his question. "Halloo, man! what is the matter? What do you see? What has come over you?"

The dreaming tailor had suddenly uttered a long, deep sigh. Now he opened his mouth wide, gasping for air, whilst two big tears slowly ran down his cheeks. The African patted him tenderly on the back, as if he had been a child who had got something in his windpipe, and said—

"Recollect where you are; it is bright, clear daylight! Cheer up, old boy; such a

woeful face is not at all suited to the sunshine
and the green woods."

" Oh, Sidi, Sidi! it is certainly clear daylight," sobbed the pasha; " but I cannot help
it. The sun is shining, and here I sit in the
green wood, and am as comfortable and as
happy as I never dreamt to be, neither
waking nor sleeping; but for all that it is a
great pity that I do not know whether it is
really true, and not a dream, like the palm-
trees and splendours of Damascus."

" Ye gods, to whom can I preach the
sermon of which my heart is full ? " cried
Hagebucher, who now stood before the pasha,
but with his back turned on him, and ad-
dressing the wood and the mountains. "Who
knows more of this world in which he lives,
and about his own self, than the fellow behind
me ? There they laugh and play in the sunshine as long as they are young; there they
dig up old weather-beaten stones—a dream
within a dream—and they all believe in their

toy; only this wise fellow behind me will not believe in his, and calls himself a fool! With what does he play? What does he see? The sea and the desert, palaces in the clouds, palm-tree groves, beautiful women, and gardens more lovely than can be met with on earth. All this is placed at his disposal, and —he blubbers! Oh, Täubrich, Täubrich!"

"Mahomed said, 'If you knew what I know, you would weep much and laugh little,'" dolefully sobbed the pasha; but the African quickly turned round and cried—

"Do you also know that Arab saying? What does it regard you? All the others who, either by cunning or force, try to conquer and bend to their will the Egyptian Proteus-life—and who have to wrestle with it until death—all these may pronounce those words, but you really might leave them alone. Täubrich, it is no small matter for a man who has returned from Tumurkieland to have you for a next-door neighbour, and I really must

protest against your trying to become, what
those above and those below us are pleased
to call a clear-headed and sensible being. I
tell you, Täubrich, that amongst all these,
there is not one who can firmly assert whether
his thoughts, wishes, and acts are real, and
therefore it is a great gift which has been
given to you, a favourite of the gods. But
come, let the others inspect corn-fields, laugh,
play, and dig up stones of the past; we will
steal away behind the bushes and choose our
own path. I have tried my hand at many
things since my return. I also have piled
up old stones; I have played, and wanted to
marry and have children; and finally, I have
only become a watchman over one small mis-
fortune in this ocean of general misery, and
for the present, this is quite enough for me.
Come, Täubrich, and step softly. I will do
you a great honour, and afterwards you can
add this picture to your dreams, when you
help the professor this winter with his
grammar in my stead."

He quickly preceded the pasha through the bushes, and crossed the ridge of the hill, carefully looking about him, like one who does not wish any uncalled-for person to follow or look after him. But there was no one to look after or follow the two strange friends, and they had soon reached the bottom of the valley, where they had to force their way through the dense underwood until they at last emerged on the high road to Fliegen-hausen, opposite the entrance to the little glen in which the cats'-mill was situated. Silently they pursued the narrow path which we have so often trodden in the course of this story, and then they stepped behind the hazel-nut bushes, and Hagebucher laid his left hand on the pasha's shoulder, and, pointing forward with the right, he said—

"That is the cat's-mill, Täubrich. All those that we left on the other side of the mountain know the spot as well as I do, but nobody ever comes here. This is partly by agreement, but not entirely so. That, which at first was shyness and reverence *vis-à-vis* a great sorrow, has soon become a comfortable habit, and it is best so. Oh, Täubrich, there is not a single wave that can beat against that threshold, since Major Wildberg sent me the American Consul's account of the battle of Richmond. They weep no more behind their flowers under the old crumbling roof. They sit there quietly, and all is quiet around them, for they have ceased to desire. . . ."

The little half wild garden before the mill was full of blossoming flowers. The windows in the lower floor were open, but in spite of these evident signs of life and cultivation, nothing stirred inside. Only the bees and butterflies hovered over the flowers and basked in the sunshine; only the tinkling of the drops was again heard from the black, mossy old wheel. Täubrich Pasha held the hand of the man from the Mountains of the Moon, and looked more absent and transfigured than he had ever done before. Suddenly the white Pomeranian made its appearance on the threshold, uttering a low growl; but quickly thinking better of it, he hurriedly and without barking ran through the garden up to the two listeners, where he uttered a half-joyful and half-mournful whine.

Leonhard Hagebucher bent down to caress his intelligent head, and whispered—

"Not to-day, my good old fellow. Go back, and keep good watch."

The sagacious animal shook itself, went back to the gate, and lay down in the sun.

Hagebucher turned round and said—

"Now let us go back to the living." And in a scarcely audible whisper, he added, "If you knew what I know, you would weep much and laugh little."

THE END.

PRINTED BY WILLIAM CLOWES AND SONS, LIMITED, LONDON AND BECCLES.

CPSIA information can be obtained
at www.ICGtesting.com
Printed in the USA
LVOW13s1350230718
584643LV00023B/713/P